My Sweet Home Georgia Cookbook

Find joy in sharing a table with friends and family, to celebrate these Southern favorites

TARA ROCKER

TDR BOOKS

TDR BOOKS

© Tara Rocker 2023

Photography: Roxy Stone, Jim Stone: Tytan Pictures
Additional photography (house, p. 122): Joe Tkacik
Design and editing: Janice Shay, Pinafore Press
Photo styling: Cynthia DeLoach

ISBN   979-8-218-26238-9

Library of Congress Control Number: 2023915188

Printed in Canada

To Walt
Ford, Isabelle, and Eleanor

Table of Contents

Introduction

I married Walt because he and his family fried fish like my family. I met Walt when I was twenty-five years old, and there was an immediate connection between us. My soul leapt when I first talked with him. Then he sealed the deal with the fried fish. That's how much food means to me. To give you a better idea about this cookbook, let me give you a little background.

I was raised in Savannah. Located on the coast of Georgia, it was the first city of the colony (and later state) founded in 1733 by General James Oglethorpe, under King George II of England. I attended school in Savannah, so I have marched along the city's squares in the annual Georgia Day parades on February 12, the state's Founders Day. As a debtors' colony and the first city in Georgia, people of all walks of life traveled here to set up a new life in the new world, or enter the port into this great state. This diveristy makes for a lively city in regards to commerce, food, religion, and backgrounds. So, I figure anyone from Savannah has either grown up with, or run into, a lively character, and that's a pretty good way to enjoy life. I am thankful for that.

Savannah is a port city, and Savannah's beach town, Tybee Island, is famous for many good times. The Savannah River and Intracoastal Waterway wind through barrier islands. Smaller waterways, like the Ogeechee River, flow off this grand land to create the swamps, ponds, and creeks of the Low Country. Sea creatures and animal life abound. In turn, those who enjoy the bounty of the sea and earth reap their plenty in shrimp, crabs, and fish. You find turkeys, deer, doves, and various other wild game living along the creeks and riverbeds. Living life in the outdoors is how the people of this land fed their loved ones at the city's inception, and remains a way of life today.

Currently, I live in Eatonton, my husband's home-town—a small town in central Georgia. We are raising our family here. The town has a familiarity to Savannah in the old homes, the historic town square, and the history of people who settled here over 200 years ago, looking for a new world in a new country. They, too, were believers and eternal optimists. Eatonton was on the path of Sherman's "March to the Sea" during the Civil War.

Savannah was gifted to Lincoln by Sherman because it was too beautiful to burn, and legend would have it that many of the homes and buildings in Eatonton were saved, and remain standing today, because the townspeople displayed the Masonic emblems in front of their buildings. As the Union officers passed through, those Union officers who were Masons were told to pass by those buildings.

Walt and I both come from families familiar to this way of life—enjoying the outdoors with our family over food and celebration. Relatives kept the phones busy asking, "Is your child home from college, let's cook out on the grill!" "Is it cold outside, let's roast some oysters!" "Is it warm, let's have a low country boil!" "Has someone died? I'll bring a pound cake for those too tired to cook." Food has shaped both of our lives, so it is no wonder it is fundamental to the well-being of our relationship. The food of south and middle Georgia shapes our lives, and is central to what is good, special, and worth celebrating.

Our children are the fifth generation of our family to

grow up on our street. Along these streets of Eatonton, camelias bloom in the winter and azaleas in the spring. Dogwoods paint the canopy of tall oaks. Wraparound wooden porches for sitting and "passing time" still exist to welcome neighbors to stop by and catch up on the latest local news and recipes.

Like Savannah, Eatonton also has ponds, rivers, creeks, and hunting land nearby, so there is always time for walks in the woods, fishing along the banks, and celebrating together on porches (and over football games).

Although living just over 180 miles from each other, Walt and I grew up in the same manner. And, strangely, the similarity of our lives doesn't end there—our fathers were both mayors of our hometowns, Savannah and Eatonton during the same four years!

Because food has been the backdrop of my life, ushering in a childhood with excitement and simple pleasures, I learned the meaning of true happiness around the table. Saying the blessing over Sunday lunch, reciting what we were thankful for at Thanksgiving, celebrating those we loved and the milestones of life with classic family recipes—these things sustained me.

Until they didn't.

When I turned forty, the desperation to feel love and happiness again became my prayer. I suffered the pain of deep sadness, and the pull of depression—a new and very frightening thing for me. I had been a happy child and adult, easy to laugh and join in any fun. Depression, I learned, brings uncertainty, fatigue, and a brain and soul that are deadened to the brightness that lies within each of us.

One day I looked in the mirror and wondered if the world would be better without me in it, and this terrified me. It's a moment in time I won't ever forget. I realize now that we are a gift of God—that life is a gift. But when depression grabbed hold of me, believing I was meant to be here took time, honesty, and the help of others.

My recipe for crawling out of this abyss of depression was a laundry list of tangible and intangible efforts. There was one particular day when I hid in the bathroom, crying. Walt came in, looked me in the eyes, and begged me to let him help. "Let me help you" is such a simple request—a plea, even. I knew he was worried and scared. He needed me, I needed him, and we needed help. I listened, and thank God I did. I leaned into Walt, and together we forged a way out of my darkness.

Once a little sliver of light and hope lessened the gravity of my situation, I began to read. I would sit on my porch—I needed to get outside, and I read somewhere that sunlight would ease depression. I scoured books with scientific studies of the subject. I watched self-help YouTube videos, and saw myself in the survivors. I listened, and slowly began to adopt some habits and therapies that changed my brain and soul. Reading, sunlight, exercise, prayer, medicine, and Walt helped. It all helped. But therapy really helped, let me tell you. For me, going to therapy with a God-centered counselor helped me see myself and the world around me in a more honest, compassionate, and loving way. Therapy is a lot of talking, and also a bunch of homework. And wouldn't you know it, one of my homework assignments was to write the book that I had planned to do since I was twenty-two. So, after thinking about writing this cookbook for years, here we are.

Depression is a crisis that moved my pen and stirred my soul. The Apostle Paul talks in the gospel about being thankful for affliction. Grateful, I now see this crisis as a gift, a reorganization of sorts. I feel that all parts of my being have been reorganized, allowing room for growth, healing, and creativity to blossom. We shall see. Ask me at the book signing.

For now, I am pleased and happy to offer these delicious recipes to you. Putting this book together helped me appreciate the joys of life, family, and food again. I sincerely hope you enjoy these dishes as much as I have over the years!

Along the streets of Eatonton,
camelias bloom in the winter and azaleas in the
spring. Dogwoods paint the canopy of tall oaks.
Wraparound wooden porches for sitting and
"passing time" still exist to welcome neighbors
to stop by and catch up on the latest
local news and recipes.

Fried Bream

For all you new fishermen who would like to serve bream at your fish fry, you need advice and a pond. My suggestion is for you to call someone you know up the road with a pond, and ask if they can take you fishing for the first time. They will show you how to bait the hook with a cricket, or a red wiggler worm. A pond fisherman will show you where the fish are biting, the time of day it's best, how to reel it in, and clean it for cooking. There are also resources online, but if I were you, reach out and ask for help. Plus, it will be a memory you won't ever forget. That's part of the special event. If you are too anxious to start before going fishing, you can usually find catfish filets already prepared for cooking at your local grocery store. You can substitute the bream with the catfish filets in this recipe. Cooking time will change from 5 minutes for a whole fish, to 2 to 3 minutes for a 4-ounce filet.

Also, if you are serving a crowd, a 4-gallon fryer (used outside) makes frying a dream (Resource Guide, p. 155).

Serves 6 to 8

2 quarts vegetable oil
14 cleaned bream
2 cups cornmeal
½ cup self-rising flour
7 teaspoons salt, divided

Add the oil to a fryer, or a deep skillet. Heat the oil to 350 degrees F.

Salt both sides of the fish with ¼ teaspoon of salt per side.

Mix the cornmeal and self-rising flour in a flat pan. Coat both sides of the fish with the dry ingredients by laying the fish in the pan and spooning the mixtures on the sides and the inside of the fish. Cover thoroughly.

Drop the fish in the heated oil and cook 5 minutes, or until they are lightly browned. The fish is finished cooking when it begins to float.

Carefull remove the fish from the oil, and let it dry on a paper bag, or a paper-towel-lined pan.

Serve hot.

I'll Marry You Fish Fry

Fried bream (pronounced "brim") and fried catfish are the seafood delicacies of ponds in the South. My grandparents, Virgina and Jimmy DeLoach, Sr., built our pond when I was seven years old. It is located in Brooklet, Georgia, just outside of Savannah and Chatham County, near the home of my grandfather and where my dad spent his childhood summers with my great-grandparents. I can remember the dam being built, and the pond being cleared. It's actually two ponds—one stocked mostly with bream, bass, and crappie, and one with catfish—but we just call it "The Pond."

Fish ponds are sought after in the South as places to relax with family and friends while enjoying the outdoors. My father-in-law has a pond set up much the same way. If you're lucky enough to have one, friends will come from near and far to fish your pond, and hopefully carry a mess of fish home for their dinner, too.

My grandmother loves to fish. She is a fine fisherman with a bass the size of a large shoebox mounted in the den of the pond house to prove it. She will spend hours on the bank throwing out her cane pole and enjoying the bounty of the earth.

It's important when hosting a fish fry for a crowd to have quite a few people fishing in order to have enough fish to eat. You can always fish ahead of time, then clean and freeze them. But as we all know, fresh is best. People can bring their own poles, or borrow the extra you have, and enjoy relaxing, talking, and catching fish. I am a member of a big family, so we always had a crowd fishing and eating. Little kids often get bored if the fish aren't biting—it's inevitable. Once when I was a child, a deacon slipped a fish on my hook when I wasn't looking, to make me believe I caught one.

My grandmother loves to fish. She is a fine fisherman with a bass the size of a large shoebox mounted in the den of the pond house to prove it. She will spend hours on the bank throwing out her cane pole, and enjoying the bounty of the earth. It takes patience to cast that pole in the water over and over again, just waiting for the bite. She would often call us and say "I've caught a bunch of fish. Y'all come on and eat."

Now remember, you have to clean the fish—this was usually my Papa's job. They set up an outdoor sink on the pond bank, with a water hose that makes the messy job of cleaning fish a little easier. The bream are scaled and the inner organs cut out. For catfish, you pull the skin back with pliers, and cut the filets off. Disclaimer: I have never cleaned a fish. I said this to Walt the other day, and he was astonished!

"You mean to tell me you're the granddaughter of Virginia DeLoach and have never cleaned a fish?" I smiled and reminded him, "That's what my Papa did."

Either way, you want to start this meal with cleaned fish. YouTube, Google, and your cousin that lives out in the country can all show you how to do this.

Eating a fried bream is a little trickier than eating a catfish filet, because you have to deal with the bones. And goodness knows, as a kid you are taught to fear the bones. I can remember my brother as a little boy thinking he had swallowed a bone. My grandmother snatched him on her lap, leaned his head back, and holding his mouth wide open, she quickly fished around the back of his mouth for the bone that was never found—but we had a laugh and a good look at his molars!

I have found the easiest way to go about eating bream is to pull the top and bottom fins out with the bones attached. Then you can eat either side of the fish easily. Finally, you have that tail. Don't be afraid to take a bite. When fried, the tail tastes like a dense, crispy chip. Try it.

The key to making a crowded fish fry successful is to relax. Remember, you are dealing with hot oil and simple ingredients. Walt's family fish fries have that very same feeling that our family's had—make it casual, make it relaxed. It's a coming together of family members and friends. Many have spent the day fishing together, and all will have tall tales to share. Walt brought me to his family fish fry the first time I met them. We had been dating for about two weeks. I knew already that I cared deeply for him, but on that day his family felt like my family. His fried fish tasted like my fried fish. That sealed the deal. I knew then that we were coming from the same place.

Hushpuppies

We always make these when we fry fish. Legend has it that when Union Soldiers were approaching, Confederate Solders would throw cooked batter balls to the dogs as they were barking, in order to keep their cover. Hence, the word "hushpuppy." The batter is the consistency of wet grainy sand. To help the hushpuppy keep it's form, use a cup of water to rinse your spoon each time before dropping it in the oil. You will notice it makes for a better and cleaner hushpuppy dough ball. The hushpuppies will turn over by themselves in the oil when one side is finished cooking. You can also move them around with a long spoon, or tongs, to keep them moving. Each hushpuppy needs to cook 2 minutes.

Makes 15 (1½-inch) hushpuppies

TANGY TARTER SAUCE
Yields just over 1¼ cup

1 cup of Duke's mayonnaise
3 tablespoons finely chopped onion
3 tablespoons sweet relish

HUSHPUPPIES
2 quarts vegetable oil
¾ cup finely chopped onion
1 cup self-rising cornmeal mix
1½ tablespoons self-rising flour
3 tablespoons sugar
¼ teaspoon salt
¼ teaspoon pepper
1 egg, beaten
¼ cup milk

To make the Tartar Sauce: Mix all ingredients in a bowl. Chill until ready to serve.

To make the Hushpuppies: Heat the oil to 350 degrees F (or use the oil from the fish fry).

Mix the cornmeal mix, self-rising flour, salt, and pepper in a medium bowl. Add the onions and mix thoroughly.

Beat one egg in separate small bowl. Beat the milk in with the egg. Pour the egg mixture into the bowl with the dry ingredients and onions and mix well.

Drop 1 generous tablespoon of the batter at a time into the oil and let them cook 2 minutes, or until golden brown.

Use a slotted spoon to remove them and transfer to a paper bag or paper-towel-lined pan to dry. Serve immediately.

Cheese Grits

Grits of all kinds are served in the South. Cheese grits happen to be my favorite, and are often served with fish for breakfast, lunch, or dinner in our neck of the woods. My Papa DeLoach would often get up early and make a big pot for all of us to enjoy upon waking. My brother followed in his footsteps, serving all my college buddies a breakfast of cheese grits when we stayed with him for a UGA football game after graduating from college. It was a blessed sight!

The cheddar cheese my Papa used is called "hoop cheese." You can identify it because it will still have the red wax on the outside portion of the wedge. I have enjoyed Parmesan and mozzarella cheese grits, sometimes flavored with garlic. Feel free to try adding these ingredients. For the fish fry, the traditional cheese grits of my childhood fits perfectly.

And, if you use Jim Dandy instant grits, you'll have them ready to eat in 5 minutes. But as is stated in "My Cousin Vinny" (filmed in Eatonton by the way, by Vinny Gambini), "So, Mr. Tipton, how could it take you five minutes to cook your grits, when it takes the entire grit-eating world twenty minutes?" Of course, Mr. Gambini was referencing the original kind, stone ground grits. So that is what I use in this recipe.

It's important to whisk in the grits when adding them to water or stock, to prevent the grits from clumping.

Serves 6 to 8

8 cups salted chicken stock
1 teaspoon salt
2 cups stone ground grits
1½ cups shredded cheddar cheese

Fill a medium pot with the stock, add the salt and bring to a boil over high heat.

Once boiling, whisk the grits into the stock. Reduce the heat to low, cover, and simmer for 20 minutes. They are done when the grits are thick and creamy.

Still on low heat, stir in the cheese until it melts thoroughly. Serve immediately.

Vinegar-Mayo Slaw

There are three types of slaw in the South that I find in most kitchens. You have sweet slaw, vinegar slaw, and a slaw like the one here that is a little sweet, with a large vinegar taste. This particular slaw is my preferred choice to serve at fish fries.

Serves 8 to 10

10 cups thinly sliced cabbage
1 cup Duke's mayonnaise
3 tablespoons apple cider vinegar
2 teaspoons pepper
1 teaspoon salt

Slice the cabbage longways to make long strands for the slaw. Add them to a large bowl, and stir in the mayonnaise and vinegar. Mix well. Stir in the salt and pepper until well combined.

Refrigerate for at least 30 minutes to let the flavors meld. If you have leftovers, it can be refrigerated, covered, for 1 day.

Key Lime Icebox Pie

My darling child Isabelle loves Key Lime Pies. This is her requested dessert at all birthdays, and every special occasion. This one has an extra special crust. It includes ginger snaps, so it can be a little stickier coming out of the refrigerator. I recommend pulling it out about 5 to 10 minutes before you plan to serve it, in order to let it loosen up a bit from the pie pan, and make it easier to serve.

Serves 8 to 10

CRUST
1 cup crushed graham crackers
1 cup crushed ginger snaps, your
    favorite brand
¼ cup sugar
8 tablespoons unsalted butter

FILLING
3 egg yolks
8 ounces cream cheese, at room
    temperature
½ cup key lime juice
1¾ cups condensed milk

Whipped cream, optional
Lime for garnish, optional

Preheat the oven to 350 degrees F.

To make the Crust: Crumble the graham crackers and ginger snaps in a food processor until finely ground. Crumble any leftover larger pieces by hand.

Add the crumbles to a large mixing bowl and stir in the sugar.

Melt the butter and pour on top of the crumble mixture. Pour the mixture in a 9-inch pie plate. Use your hands to press the crust into the bottom and up the sides of the pie plate. Once set, bake the crust in the oven for 10 minutes.

To make the Filling: Mix all of the filling ingredients in the bowl of a mixer on medium speed for 2 to 3 minutes until smooth.

Pour the pie into the crust, and cook for 15 minutes. Remove from oven and let the pie sit at room temperature for 15 minutes, then refrigerate for at least 1 hour before serving.

Top with whipped cream, or a slice of lime for garnish.

New Year's Day
Goodness and Good Luck

I knew that we had my parents' approval as a married couple when Walt and I first hosted our parents and a few close friends for New Year's Day lunch. My father admitted, "That is the best meal I have ever had in your kitchen!" I have to confess, it wasn't all me. I'm blessed with a talented husband—Walt can really cook, and we enjoy making great food together.

New Year's Day lunch has always been a tradition in our family. The crowd size has changed, and the lead chef of the day usually depends on where you are spending your holidays, but I don't think I ever had a New Year's day meal that didn't include black-eyed peas, pork, and at least some sort of greens, (though it took me a few years to come around on the greens part)—all meant to ensure, according to Southern tradition, that I would have good luck and prosperity in the New Year.

Growing up and living on land that has seen the ravages of the Civil War is prevalent if you look around at the historical buildings and writings, and listen to the tales. The reason we eat black-eyed peas for good luck comes from the Civil War South. That is the only crop that the Yankees didn't burn, because they thought it was only good for the livestock. Southerners learned to cook and eat the black-eyed peas and, therefore, felt they brought luck to them, since the Yankees didn't starve them out. Black-eyed peas are a sign of fortitude in the South.

MENU

Pork Backbone and Rice

Turnip and Mustard Greens

Walt's Black-Eyed Peas

Skillet Cornbread

Spiced Tea

Grandmother's Chocolate Stack Cake

Many of our traditional dishes are deeply rooted in the South, with the influence of African American culture—and especially the Gullah Geechee cooking of this region of the South.

So, yes, you must eat these foods on this day or you are doomed, or so we believe in the South. I'm skeptical, but you won't see me testing this tradition. I realize we're also participating in the memories and history of people of all backgrounds, religions, and cultures raised in this land.

Both Walt and I grew up with Soul Food in abundance, and readily available. Many of the traditional dishes deeply rooted in the South can be traced to the influence of African American culture—and especially the Gullah Geechee cooking of this region. It was this culture that introduced the rice, sweet potatoes, okra, and other staples of Southern Soul cooking that we enjoy now.

For decades in Savannah, Elizabeth's on 37th was our most popular fine dining restaurant, and on the cutting edge of making Southern food a recognized cuisine. I had the great fortune to know the Terry family, who ran the restaurant and lived above it for the time I knew them. Celeste, their daughter, was in my class at Country Day School, and became a good friend. Her parents generously opened their doors to their children's classmates for fine dining "on the house."

As a senior at Country Day, we were offered the opportunity to spend a month working in a career of our choice for a final pass-fail grade before graduation. I chose to be in the kitchen at Elizabeth's, because I looked forward to hosting parties, and knew I could learn a lot from the best kitchen and chef in Savannah. For a month I first prepped vegetables for dinner service, and next worked with the pastry chef. I learned how to cut vegetables consistently, why convection is important, and how to crack an egg with one hand. Most of all, I observed Southern cuisine and hospitality at its finest. For me, this is what this book is all about, whether you are cooking for family, or a hungry crowd.

This New Year's Day, and for all those that follow, I wish you good luck and prosperity. Be sure to cook up your peas, pork, and greens so all your dreams will come true.

Pork Back Bone and Rice

I love to serve this dish with Southern chow-chow or pear relish (Resource Guide, p. 155). It is also a great one-pot meal for dinner or Sunday lunch. Be aware when browning the pork in the pot, that it is ready to turn when it will release from the pan. If it is sticking, let it cook another minute more. Sometimes you have to ask your butcher for pork back bone. However, bone-in country style ribs are a great substitute. Just be sure to include the bone. Note that when the pork is finished boiling, you will have broth left over. Use this liquid to cook the rice.

Serves 8 to 10

1 (2½ to 3 pound) pork back bone (or bone-in country style ribs, if back bone isn't available)
1 tablespoon olive oil
1½ cups chopped onion
Pinch of salt
4 cloves garlic, minced
3 cups long grain white rice
1½ teaspoons salt
1 teaspoon pepper

Salt and Pepper the back bone thoroughly.

Heat the olive oil in an 8-quart lidded pot or Dutch oven over medium-high heat. Add the backbone and cook 3 to 5 minutes on all sides, until browned. Once browned, remove the meat to a plate to rest at room temperature.

Add the onion to the pan with a pinch of salt, and cook 3 to 5 minutes, until the onion is translucent and has begun to brown on the edges. Then add the garlic and cook for 2 minutes, or until fragrant. (After 2 minutes garlic will burn and become bitter.)

Deglaze the pan by pouring in 1 cup water, and using a spatula or straight wooden spoon to scrape all the bits of goodness off the bottom of the pan.

Once deglazed, add the pork and any juices that collected on the plate back into the pot. Cover the pork with 7 more cups of water, and bring to a low boil over medium-high heat, with the pot partially covered. Cook for 1 hour, or until the meat is fork tender.

Once the pork is done, place it in a plate or bowl and allow the meat to cool a bit.

In a separate bowl, capture all the broth left in the pot. Measure out 6 cups of this broth you need to next make the rice. If you don't have enough broth to make 6 cups, add water.

Return the pork to the empty pot, and add the 6 cups of broth. Stir in the salt and pepper. Bring to a boil and add 3 cups of uncooked rice. Cover and simmer on low for 20 minutes.

Serve immediately.

Turnip and Mustard Greens

The key to cooking turnips and mustard greens is you must wash, wash, and wash them again. The best way to do this is to fill a sink with water as you de-stem and swirl the greens around. Fill and rinse the greens in the sink at least three times, washing the sink down after each rinse. You will know the greens are clean when there is not any grit or sand in the bottom of the sink after you let the water drain.

This is imperative, because a little grit goes a LONG way.

Serves 10 to 12 --

2 pounds fresh turnip greens, cleaned and de-stemmed

2 pounds fresh mustard greens, cleaned and de-stemmed

3 fresh turnip roots, peeled and washed

¾ pound cured ham hock

¾ pound sliced salt pork

¼ pound fat back

Thouroughly rinse and de-stem the turnip and mustard greens (see notes above).

Peel the turnip roots and cut into quarters.

In a large pot or Dutch oven over medium-high heat, add the ham hock, salt pork, and fat back. Brown and render the fat, stirring occasionally, for 10 minutes.

With the meat in the pot, lower the heat to medium, and add the greens to the pot. Cover, and stir occasionally, for 10 minutes, keeping the greens covered when not stirring. The leaves will wilt considerably.

After 10 minutes, add the turnip roots, cover, and continue to cook another 10 minutes.

Next, pour 8 cups of water into the pot, and increase the heat to high, bringing all the ingredients to a boil. Once boiling, reduce the heat to low and simmer for 1½ hours until the meat is tender and the greens are fully cooked.

Walt's Black-Eyed Peas

As you can tell, New Year's Day lunch is a big deal. Walt joined me in cooking the lunch the year we arrived home on December 31st from a whirlwind trip to Disney World with our three young kids. We were exhausted, but traditions must carry on! He offered to make these peas, and I am so happy he did. He brought the taste up ten levels! Peas can become mushy if not properly executed. These are almost a meal all their own. I love to serve them over the rice in the Pork Back Bone and Rice recipe.

Serves 10 to12

16 ounces dried black-eyed peas
¾ pound hog jowl, sliced into bite-sized
    pieces, available at your local butcher
¾ pound ham hock
2 cups onions, coarsely chopped
1 quart salted beef stock
1 quart unsalted beef stock
¾ teaspoon pepper

Soak the black-eyed peas overnight, then rinse, and drain.

Slice the hog jowl into bite-size pieces and place in a pot with the ham hock over medium-high heat. Cook 5 minutes, long enough for it to render and brown.

Reduce the heat to medium, add the chopped onions, and cook 6 to 8 minutes until they turn translucent.

Pour the drained peas into the pot with the all the ingredients, increase the heat to medium-high and cook for 5 minutes.

Stir in both quarts of beef stock, and bring to a boil. Once boiling, lower the heat and let the ingredients simmer for 40 to 45 minutes, until the peas are tender.

Be sure not to overcook, as the peas will turn to mush.

Stir in the pepper once peas reach the desired tenderness.

Skillet Cornbread

In my Grandaddy Cheney's later years, he became an expert in cornbread. For a man that never did a tremendous amount of cooking, he mastered this. The key, I learned, is that it is imperative to properly heat the oil in the skillet before pouring in the batter. This is only way to ensure your cornbread will have a proper crust.

Serves 8 to 10

1½ cups buttermilk
⅓ cup vegetable oil in the skillet, plus ¼ cup vegetable oil for the batter
1 large egg
2 cups self-rising buttermilk cornmeal mix

Preheat the oven to 400 degrees F.

To properly heat an 8-inch cast iron skillet, add ⅓ cup vegetable oil and heat for 10 minutes in the oven.

In a bowl, whisk all ingredients together until smooth, and pour into the heated skillet. The batter will bubble and form a crust in the hot oil as it is poured.

Bake for 20 minutes, or until golden brown and firm in the middle. Let it cool slightly before cutting.

Spiced Tea

This is a wonderful drink to keep simmering on the stove during cool days and holidays, to share with your loved ones. It smells divine. It also serves nicely in a warm crock pot. It will keep in your refrigerator for up to five days. This recipe is great for a big holiday crowd, but can be halved for personal use.

Makes 20 to 25 cups

5 family-size tea bags, your favorite brand black tea
2 whole cinnamon sticks
1 tablespoon whole cloves
2 cups sugar
1 (46-ounce) can unsweetened pineapple juice
Juice and pulp of 3 oranges
Juice and pulp of 3 lemons

In a large pot or saucepan over high heat, bring 8 cups of water to a boil. Add the tea bags, remove from the heat, cover, and steep for 5 minutes.

Secure the cinnamon sticks and cloves in a cheesecloth tied with twine, and add to the tea.

After the tea has steeped, add another 5 cups water, and stir in the sugar, pineapple, orange, and lemon juice and pulp.

Bring the mixture again to a boil for 10 minutes.

Remove from heat, and discard the cheesecloth items.

Serve warm. This tea may be kept, refrigerated, in a lidded container for 5 days.

Grandmother's Chocolate Stack Cake

This is my favorite cake from my childhood and still today. The tiny cake layers with fudge like icing make for a delicious dessert. My Grandmother DeLoach would often make this cake for my birthday. One of my life goals was to learn how to make this cake so I could share it with my family. Now you can share it with yours!

I use three cake pans for my cake, each with a 9-inch diameter. I cook two batches of layers.

A note on the icing, be sure your icing is warm when you spread it on the layers coming out of the oven. It helps the cake to absorb all the chocolate goodness. Plus, it spreads beautifully.

Serves 12 to 14

ICING
3 cups of sugar
18 ounces evaporated milk
2 tablespoons of butter
⅓ cup powdered cocoa
1 tablespoon vanilla

CAKE
3 cups of cake flour sifted
1 tablespoon baking powder
1 cup of butter
2 cups of sugar
4 eggs
1 cup of sour cream
1 cup of milk

Preheat your oven to 350 degrees F.

To make the Icing: melt the sugar, evaporated milk, butter, cocoa, and vanilla in a saucepan over medium-high heat for 20 minutes. It will begin to bubble and slowly boil. Stir constantly to keep the icing from scorching and to bring the ingredients together.

After 20 minutes, remove from heat and set aside to cool.

To make the Cake: sift the flour with the baking powder in a mixing bowl.

Cream the butter and sugar in a mixer on medium speed. Add the eggs and continue to mix well. Next, add the flour and sour cream alternately, mixing well until the batter is smooth.

The cake is baked in 6 small layers, in 3 cakepans, used twice. First, grease 3 (9-inch) cake pans with a spray of Baker's Joy all around, including the edges. Then pour the batter to a ¼-inch depth to cover the bottom of the pans.

Bake the layers for 17 to 20 minutes. Multiple pans can be baked at one time if the oven will accommodate them. Repeat until all 6 layers are baked. If you bake in batches, begin to ice the tops of the layers as they come from the oven.

To ice, place the first layer on the cake plate. Using 2-3 tablespoons of icing, cover the top of that layer, and place an un-iced layer atop of it. Repeat until all layers are iced. When the top layer is ready, add an abundance of icing to allow some to drip down the sides. If you like, smooth the icing around the side of the cake to cover. When fully iced, let it sit for 30 minutes before serving.

Planning Tips for Parties

I would like to offer a few tips that will make your life easier, whether you are planning family dinners, parties, or small get-togethers. Keep in mind, the advice below is good for any event.

1. Set your table a day before the party. This will give you time to gather all the dishes, linens, and decorations needed. It saves you time on the day of the dinner, and is a welcome sight for the guests upon arrival.

2. When hosting outdoors, set your various tables and chairs up a day in advance, if possible. Linens and flowers can be put out in the hours leading up to the event.

3. If you are ordering any items online, plan for them to be delivered ten days or so before the dinner so you can decide if they will work, or if you need to find a better option. How many times can you not find an ingredient you need on the day of the party? This solves that problem.

4. In a similar way, buy your grocery store dry goods and staples one or two days before you cook and serve, to assure they are handy when you are to prepare the dishes.

5. Check your recipes to see if you might save time by pre-prepping, or preparing any dishes ahead that could be refrigerated or frozen until the day of the dinner. Remember to pull anything that needs to thaw early on the day of the dinner, or move it to the refrigerator section the night before.

6. Wash out any coolers needed the day or two before the event. If needed, remember to buy ice!

7. Stock your drinks and bar early the day of the party so those items can be chilling on the ice.

Low Country Boil,
No Linens Required

It's obvious *les fruits de la mer* are special guests and time-honored traditions on tables along the Georgia coast. Living in the Low Country, you can "get on the shrimp" at various times of the year. And by "get on," I mean you have found your spot to fish for that day's abundant catch. Shrimp season runs from June until December, making fall a great time to shrimp in Georgia.

One such fall, when Walt and I were living in Savannah, we planned to go fishing. We took our little 13-foot Whaler out, and realized that the shrimp were jumping. I mean *actually* jumping out of the water, just asking to be caught. Because the tide was low and the water was just below the line of marsh grass, the shrimp were all stirred up. They had congregated along the marsh shoreline waiting for the tide to bring them up and push them in, and they were jumping to get into that marsh to feed, but to no avail. Happily, we had arrived just in time to catch dinner, and then some, for that evening.

So we stored the fishing rods, and wheeled around to pick up a large cooler and cast net. Walt called a buddy to come help, so I could drive the boat while they both caught shrimp.

For the next few hours, I took the boat up into the marsh right where the shrimp were jumping, and they threw the cast net and dumped loads of shrimp into our cooler. That evening was one of those times when you happily call your buddies and say, "Fellas, I was on the shrimp today. We're having a

Low Country Boil tonight on the dock." Then you scoop up your river water, throw in your Low Country Boil ingredients—shrimp with the heads on for this occasion, smoked sausage, corn, and potatoes—have a few beers and enjoy the sunset while it cooks, then pour it out on the table, and dinner is served.

This is another one of those country-casual events that we love so well in the South. I attended many as a child, but the first Low Country Boil I helped to host was at my parents' house when I was about to graduate from college. They were traveling and had allowed that I could host a small get-together while they were out of town. I was so excited! This would be the very first Low Country Boil organized somewhat on my own.

My older cousin offered to cook the food and bring the pot, if I would have the porch ready and the food in the fridge. Done! So, the entire night before, I searched through Mother's linens looking for just the right color cloth napkin to put out with the casual silverware. I had perfected the perfect play list of Norah Jones and some others. Well, Lynn Tootle, my cousin, and Vanessa, his girlfriend (now wife), arrived at the house ready to cook. Lynn looked at the cloth linens and silverware and asked in wonderment, "What's that?"

What's what, I thought? He pointed to the linens and said, "We don't need all that. We need newspapers and paper towels." So I quickly gathered up all the pretty napkins and silverware and pulled out yesterdays' newspaper to cover the back porch table, and rolls of paper towels to use as napkins and cleanup. Dinner was poured on the back porch at sunset, and a great time was had by all—even without my mother's pretty linens!

When we moved to central Georgia from Savannah, coming across fresh shrimp became a little more difficult. Enter crawfish, which was a new crustacean for me. Walt actually prefers a crawfish boil over a Low Country boil, but they're both great. The best time to have a crawfish boil is March through May. During

Lynn looked at the cloth linens and silverware and asked in wonderment, "What's that?" What's what, I thought? He pointed to the linens, "We don't need all that. We need newspapers and paper towels."

this season you can call a crawfish place in Louisiana (Resource Guide, p. 155) and have live crawfish delivered to your house 24 hours later—live crawfish, seasoning, and you even get Mardi-Gras beads in the box!

Most everything is cooked and eaten similarly with these two boils—sausage, potatoes, corn, drawn butter, and cocktail sauce. However, shrimp and crawfish are eaten entirely differently. Most people know how to peel a shrimp. Most shrimp that you buy already have the heads off, so all you do is pinch the tail off and peel off the outer casing.

Now, crawfish are a little different because the head is usually on, and they have a tough exoskeleton. You pinch the head off and suck the flavoring out—don't worry, it tastes great. Then you must bend the tail backwards and peel the hard casing off the crawfish meat. That is where the goodie is, and where the sustenance is located. Walt thinks that crawfish have much more flavor than shrimp, but I think both are fantastic.

Either way, there is no place for Mother's linens. Save those for the New Year's Day Luncheon.

Low Country Boil

For our purposes, I'm going to teach you to prepare a Low Country Boil. You can add crawfish if you like, or omit. Our crawfish resource is The Louisiana Crawfish Company. Call them and you can have mudbugs overnighted right to your door. All the instructions and ingredients you need will be included in the package. Additionally, you will need much more water to cook crawfish than you will for shrimp. So consider that when preparing. I also recommend 17 quarts of water for a crawfish boil, with the following ingredients, but with 10 to 12 pounds of crawfish instead of 3 pounds of shrimp.

Key point for either boil: Do not cut your potatoes. Cutting the skin makes the water—and all the food that follows—slimy. The smaller red potatoes work well for this reason.

One method of serving is to transfer the boil to a pot or cooler, and let people serve themselves. You can be sure a well-rounded plate will be made, and a lot of sauce served. I find more vegetables are eaten when people make their own plate. Just keep this in mind.

Another method of serving a crowd is to pour all the ingredients out on a table covered with newspaper, and let people stand around and eat. At these times, people are going to go for the shrimp first, sausage second, then the corn and potatoes last. Be sure to only pour out what you are sure will be eaten. You can always refresh the table from the cooler.

And don't forget to have drawn butter and cocktail sauce available for dipping. My sister-in-law also loves to have honey to dip her sausage in.

Serves 6, and can be doubled

½ cup Zatarain's Pro Boil seasoning, or
   your choice seafood seasoning
2 pounds petite red potatoes
2 pounds Roger Wood sausage links, cut
   in 3-inch lengths
6 ears corn, cut in thirds
3 pounds fresh shrimp, de-headed
1 cup drawn butter (recipe, opposite page)
2 cups cocktail sauce (recipe, opposite
   page)

Add 6 quarts of water to a large stockpot along with the Zatarain's seasoning, and bring it to a boil over high heat.

Once boiling, add the potatoes. Drop them in whole and cook for 10 minutes. After 10 minutes, add the sausage and let it cook for 5 minutes. Then drop in the corn, and let cook for another 10 minutes, bringing the water back to a boil.

After the final 10 minutes of cooking, add the shrimp and turn the heat off. Swirl the shrimp around with a spoon for 2 minutes until they turn pink, then remove from the heat, and let everything soak for 3 minutes and cool slightly.

Now it is time to eat!

Use a strainer basket to transfer the Low Country Boil from the pot into a cooler, or serve directly onto newspaper or plates.

Drawn Butter

1 pound unsalted butter

Bring the butter to a boil in a saucepan. After 5 to 7 minutes, the boiling will begin to slow and the foam reduces. At this point, pour the butter in a glass dish. The milk solids will settle in the bottom of the bowl. Spoon the liquid butter from the top into a serving bowl.

Cocktail Sauce

Yields approximately 2 cups, and can be doubled

1½ cups ketchup
3 tablespoons prepared horseradish
3 tablespoons lemon juice
1 tablespoon Worcestershire sauce
1 teaspoon hot sauce
½ teaspoon celery salt
½ teaspoon onion powder

Mix the ingredients in a small bowl, and chill for at least 20 minutes before serving.

Sweet Tea

No one escapes the heat in the South on a summer day—not even our animals! The number one human refreshment in the sweltering heat is sweet tea. It's lovely, garnished with sprigs of mint, or a wedge of lemon. There's a longstanding national debate over which is best: sweet or unsweet? Both are good on a hot day, but the combination of cold and sweet can't be beat, in my book.

Makes 2 quarts

5 family-size black tea bags, your
    favorite brand
1¼ cups sugar

Add the tea bags to 8 cups of water in a saucepan. Bring to a boil over high heat, then reduce the heat to low and simmer for 5 minutes.

Pour the tea into a two-quart pitcher. Add the water and sugar, and stir until the sugar is dissolved.

Pour into a glass over ice.

Decadent Dark Chocolate Brownies

These are great alone, or served with Cinnamon Ice Cream (recipe, p. 82) and berries.

Makes 16 brownies

4 tablespoons butter, room temperature
½ cup sugar
½ cup brown sugar
2 eggs
1 teaspoon vanilla
3 tablespoons vegetable oil
½ teaspoon salt
½ cup all-purpose flour
½ cup dark chocolate cocoa powder
⅔ cup dark chocolate morsels
¼ teaspoon kosher salt

Preheat the oven to 350 degrees F.

Cream the butter and sugar in a large bowl until well mixed.

Add the eggs, vanilla, and vegetable oil and mix well.

Add the salt, flour, and cocoa powder and mix well.

Gently fold the dark chocolate morsels into the batter.

Grease an 8 x 8-inch glass baking dish, and pour the brownie mixture in.

Bake for 30 to 35 minutes, or until a toothpick placed in the middle comes out clean.

Once finished cooking, set the pan aside to cool slightly, then sprinkle lightly with kosher salt.

Feel Good Food For The Soul

When you think of comfort food

I am sure certain memories flood your mind. Is it a trip to the Waffle House, your mother's home-cooked biscuits, or your favorite bowl of soup? To me comfort food means those meals you enjoy when your heart needs a pick-me-up. You seek them out to be reminded of the comforts of home and familiarity. The meals are unique to each person. I know you have one too, and I bet your mother or grandmother might have something to do with them!

My family is at its best when comfort food recipes are needed. If you aren't feeling well, out comes the potato peeler. Mother is going to whip up her potato soup. This is the end-all, be-all of soups that satisfy your soul and stop your sniffles. And now I make the same soup for my children when they are under the weather. I hope it will be just as satisfying for yours.

MENU

Potato Soup

Cheesy Toast

*Grandaddy's
Cure-all Cookies*

One of the best things about this potato soup is how simple it is. For those times when you aren't feeling well, it's so satisfying not to have to cook much in order to get a good meal. When Walt and I first started dating, I got terribly sick. All I wanted was some potato soup. Walt, being the kind and fabulous cook that he is, went straight to work. He made the most decadent potato soup—full of cream, bacon bits, and sprinkled with green onions. It was lovely, but I could hardly eat it. I felt bad for Walt, but it was just too rich. I needed my mother's version. The bacon grease was still in the pot and I couldn't dare smell it, so I called her and asked her if she would please come over and wash my dishes and make some simple potato soup? Of course, she did just that. The simple familiarity of childhood food is perfect at these times and, frankly, there's nothing Southern about that. It must be universal.

At times, when I felt exhausted or bewildered and could not figure out what to eat, a cheeseburger often became the menu item of the day. It was familiar, tasty, and easy to make. In college, on Sunday nights, after Chi Omega chapter spent with my college buddies, a cheeseburger was often my go-to choice. I missed my family a little on those days. The need for comfort food was also responsible for the occasional two a.m. late night run to The Grill in Athens, and visits to the Varsity after doctor appointments, when Walt and I were expecting our third child.

Such was the case during the quarantine lockdown of 2020. The worry in having to shelter in place, and whether to wear a mask, or not to wear a mask—what a difficult time of our lives! Many will never forget, and many future generations will be regaled with what we experienced.

I can honestly say that those first few weeks of March 2020 were some of the most bewildering and frightening, fearing for the health of our family as a whole. I imagine much of the world would agree. Supplies were low and the threat of disease real. My stress level was extremely high. Decision-making was difficult. Fortunately, we live in rural Georgia so supplies were easier to come by, and we could get out and move around in our yard. Like many other families, we adapted to teaching children from home, and preparing three home-cooked meals daily for our family of five. To be perfectly honest, all this cooking overwhelmed me at first. I even developed carpal tunnel syndrome. I was preparing everyone just what they wanted, and quickly learned that I would never be able to customize all the meals. I had to streamline the process and prepare one type of meal for breakfast, lunch, and dinner. The short order cook had to go.

Because decision making was difficult for me due to extreme anxiety, all I could think of was cheeseburgers for dinner. I was so overwhelmed by the world coming to an end, that all I could cook for dinner was this familiar comfort food, that was easy to make. And since we were home all the time, lighting up the charcoal grill wasn't a big deal. We had time. And ground beef was readily available. For the first few weeks, we had cheeseburgers probably two or three nights a week, and leftovers for lunch on the other days. After a few weeks of this, we realized we weren't going back to normal any time soon, and Walt looked at me and said, "We're going to have to expand the menu around here. We can't eat cheeseburgers for every meal."

My aptly-named Quarantine Cheeseburger would also be the first meal that I prepared for friends when the world started to open back up. It was June 5, 2020, and we decided that we were going to have a few close friends and their kids over to eat, as we hadn't seen each other since the shutdown. The kids and I were cleaning up the house in a fury because this dinner was a last-minute decision. I sent the kids upstairs to clean the rooms when we felt the house shake. We live in an old house in downtown Eatonton, so when the

The simple familiarity of childhood food is perfect at these times and, frankly, there's nothing Southern about that. It must be universal.

kids jump off their beds or off the furniture it shakes the house and makes the windows rattle. I was picking up the pillows in the den and felt the shake and just assumed someone was jumping off the bed. I let it go.

Right after the shake, Walt called me in a panic yelling through the phone "Are you alright? Are you and the kids alright?" Startled, I kind of yelled back, "Of course, what are you talking about?"

He said, "Tara, you are going to think I am crazy, but something just fell out of the sky!"

Stunned, I couldn't imagine what he was talking about. I would soon learn that a plane had exploded a few miles from our house, and crashed just outside of town. In a split-second, what we thought was going to be a night of fun and reunion became a nightmare for a family traveling above our small community, as well as the members of our community trying to help.

That night our friends did come over for dinner—all but one, Cooper Rainey, who was the coroner working on this terrible accident.

It was a long day and night for Cooper, but we were able to finally able to feed our friend. It was a cheeseburger. He was quiet. We were too. In that very strange year, we were yet again reminded that it is often not what you are cooking that matters, but rather finding comfort in breaking bread and being together around the table.

A few of those comfort foods are included in this chapter. These things have nourished me, and have brought me to the table to find conversation and community. First is the simple potato soup of my childhood. If you would like to "square up" this meal, you can always pair the soup with any of the other soup recipes in this book for a dinner with soup choices for your guests. Additionally, this soup would go great with grilled steak or grilled chicken, and you could add a simple salad to round out your meal.

Potato Soup
(with a heaping side of love)

Mother always uses Russet potatoes for this soup, and so do I.

Serves 6 ---

8 cups Russet potatoes, peeled and
   chopped into 1-inch cubes
2 tablespoons butter
1 teaspoon salt
¼ cup flour
1¼ cups milk
¼ teaspoon pepper

Place the potato cubes in a large pot with 6 cups water, and add the butter and salt. Bring to a boil over high heat, then reduce the heat to medium and cook 8 to 10 minutes, or until the potatoes are fork tender.

Whisk the flour and milk together in a small bowl until smooth. Using a strainer and a whisk, pour the mixture through the strainer into the pot of the cooking potatoes, whisking as it goes in. This allows the flour to cook and combine smoothly with the soup. Reduce the heat to low and simmer for 20 minutes, stirring often, to cook the flour. Add the pepper. To increase the thickness, you can mash up some of the potatoes.

Serve immediately.

Cheesy Toast

1 whole baguette, or whole loaf of
   your choice
8 tablespoons butter, melted
8 ounces extra sharp white cheddar,
   grated
¼ teaspoon pepper

Heat the oven broiler.

Slice the loaf into pieces, 1-inch thick.

Brush both sides of the bread with butter.

Place on a cookie sheet and broil both sides 1 to 2 minutes, until lightly toasted.

Sprinkle cheese on the top of each slice. Broil just 1 minute, until melted and bubbly.

Remove and sprinkle with pepper before serving.

Grandaddy's Cure-All Cookies

This was my Grandaddy Cheney's favorite cookie. They are one of mine, too. For a twist, Granny would sometimes replace the chocolate morsels with raisins. The dough can be kept in the freezer for up to three months.

Yields 3 to 4 dozen

1 cup butter
1 cup light brown sugar
1 cup granulated sugar
2 eggs, plus 1 yolk
1 teaspoon vanilla extract
3 cups self-rising flour, sifted
1 cup Rice Krispies cereal
1 cup Quick Oats
1 cup sweetened coconut
1 to 2 cups coarsely chopped pecans
1 cup semi-sweet chocolate
   morsels, divided

Preheat the oven to 325 degrees F.

In the bowl of a mixer, cream the butter, brown sugar, and granulated sugar on low until smooth.

Add the eggs and yolk, and the vanilla extract, and mix on low speed until just combined.

Add the flour in 3 increments, mixing after each addition until combined.

Fold in the Rice Krispies and oats until just combined.

Fold in the coconut and pecans.

Finally, fold in ¾ cup of chocolate morsels.

Cover a cookie sheet with parchment.

Scoop 1 heaping tablespoon of batter per cookie, and place each scoop 2 inches apart on the parchment.

Press the remaining chocolate chips on top of the dough balls, about 2 to 3 chips per cookie.

Bake for 12 to 14 minutes, until the edges begin to brown and the middle is still a lighter color.

Remove, and set aside to cool on a rack.

Any Day
Summer Supper

Oh, I love the joys of summer—the freedom of a more relaxed schedule, a summer vacation, plus all the fresh produce you grow or buy during those months—tomatoes, corn, watermelon, peaches, and peas.

When I was growing up, we lived on a dirt road with a dead end. I was always offended that my road was referred to as a "dead end," but the stories of my early barefooted childhood adventures began here. My neighborhood gang was comprised of about ten children that met to play in our "club" just across the street in the woods.

If you looked closely, the entrance to the club still remains. Two tree branches form a canopy and doorway, just high enough for anyone shorter than five feet to enter. It ushered us into our own den under the shelter of the tree. An area that had been worn down by our footsteps and games of chase formed a kind of circle around the tree. It was here where we had meeting days and cleanup days. We took pride in our club, and would clean away any branches that fell in the way of our games, wandering in the woods and pretending to be spies.

It is where I chopped the tail off a snake, got endless redbug bites, and where I learned to pick blackberries on the side of the road. This dead end was full of life for us kids!

MENU

3-2-1 Biscuits

—

Fresh Tomato and Cucumber Salad

—

Fried Pork Chops

—

Summer Field Peas

—

Squash Casserole

—

Lemonade

—

Cinnamon Ice Cream

—

On one of our adventures we got lost in the woods beyond the dead end road, where the woods met the farmland of the surrounding area. Our parents were always confident that the biggest threat to our safety was mischievousness, so we were free to roam. One day while we were playing, we found ourselves deep in the woods. We couldn't see above the pasture grass and overgrown area where we were walking, so we didn't know where we were. I was the oldest and the tallest, so in order to keep everyone together, I had each younger child pick up a big stick and walk with it through the woods so that I could see them. Everyone was nervous and a little frightened, but we just knew we were on the adventure of our lives. We walked in a line, one behind the other, with one of the older kids bringing up the rear to be sure no man was left behind. We marched and marched for what seemed like all afternoon but, truthfully, it was about twenty minutes.

Finally, we walked out of the tall pasture grass and could see Mr. Rollins' farm and cornfield. We were thrilled that we found our way through the woods and now had a point of origin, and knew how to get back home. What a sense of empowerment—and you can bet our appetites were good that evening!

Memories of summer suppers impact the things I do now as a wife and mother, too. Summer means having a little bit more time to pull together a meal that is reminiscent of the tastes and smells of my childhood. Other seasons are full and busy from sunup to sundown, what with carrying kids to school, events, and sports, and trying to fit shopping into the schedule. The chores of summer include picking fresh tomatoes or peppers from the garden, or picking up local produce and coming home to cook it that night. To this day my favorite tomatoes are my father-in-law's, homegrown in our yard.

The Cherokee Purple and Kellogg's Breakfast tomato varieties are best grown from seedlings. Allowing them to fully ripen on the vine allows the sweet and acidic flavors to dominate. And never, ever, put them in the refrigerator, or you will end up with a mushy, mealy tomato. Vine ripe, red, and at room temperature is the best.

Summer gives us a little more time to slow down a bit, and it brings us together around the table more often. Having the time to pick peaches off the tree, and bring them home for peach cobbler is a dream come true. My Granny and Grandaddy Cheney lived a few miles down from us during the latter years of their lives. Granny would often cook dinner for us during this season of her life. She took time and great care to make even a summer supper special, with layers of fine linens, glass coasters for cold glasses of iced tea, and the freshest vegetables. Regardless of what's served, or who prepares it, you can always taste the time and love that is put into a meal. I learned that when Granny made us summer suppers. This summer supper embodies a little more time, and a whole lot more goodness.

Regardless of what's served, or who prepares it, you can always taste the time and love that is put into a meal.

3-2-1 Biscuits

There are countless biscuit recipes in the South. I like this recipe because it is tasty, easy to make, and easy to remember the main ingredient amounts: 3 flour, 2 milk, and 1 butter. So if you are off on a weekend with friends, and in charge of breakfast, this is a quick go-to. I encourage you to use a big handful of flour to dust your surface before rolling out the dough. It will help you handle the dough more easily. Be sure not to handle the dough too much though, so that the biscuits turn out light. And don't worry, the dough is supposed to be lumpy. Lastly, I use a 3-inch diameter biscuit cutter, or glass tumbler, to cut out these big puppies.

Makes 12 to 14

3 cups self-rising flour, plus extra
   for dusting
1 stick (8 tablespoons) cold butter, cubed
2 cups buttermilk, divided
¼ cup butter melted
Baker's Joy, or other non-stick baking
   spray

Optional: a drizzle of honey

Preheat the oven to 500 degrees F.

Pour the flour in a large bowl, and make a well in the center. Add the cubed butter and 1 cup of the buttermilk. Use a fork to cut the the butter and buttermilk into the flour. Mix until all the ingredients are incorporated, and the dough is wet and lumpy.

Dust a flat surface with a handful of flour. Pour the dough out onto the floured surface and pat down until the dough is ½-inch thick.

Spray a cookie sheet with Baker's Joy. Use a jar or a cookie cutter to cut the biscuits, and place them on a sheet pan. Incorporate any leftover dough into biscuits and add them to the sheet pan.

Place the pan in the oven and cook for 5 minutes, then reduce the heat to 425 degrees F, and cook for 10 more minutes to finish. The biscuits are ready when they are golden brown.

Brush the top of each biscuit with the melted butter and serve while still warm. I'm drizzling Lee's Bees honey (Resource Guide, p. 155) on the warm biscuits shown here in the photo, and I highly recommend doing so, if you prefer your biscuits sweet.

Fresh Tomato and Cucumber Salad

My Papa DeLoach taught me how to cut a tomato when I was about 11 years old. I loved tomatoes and he wanted to be sure I knew the proper technique. I can still hear him say, "Now Michelle, (my middle name and what he always called me) you take the tomato like this, and you put it on the plate here. Then you grab your knife and just slice it right on through. Nothin' to it! Cut the stem off. And the end. Slice it right on up. Nothin' finer a-tall!"

This is a great salad to serve in the summer when fresh tomatoes and cucumbers abound. Use a spoon to scrape the seeds out of the cucumber. When you slice the cucumbers, they will turn into lovely half-moon shapes. I used an English Cucumber for this recipe, but any cucumber will work. This is a nice salad to serve slightly chilled, if you have time. However, don't chill for too long or your tomatoes will turn mushy and mealy.

Serves 6 to 8 --

2 cups vine ripe tomatoes, cut in ½-inch wedges

1 cup cucumber, seeded and sliced in ¼-inch half-rounds

¼ cup red onions, cut in thinly-sliced half-rounds

2 tablespoons olive oil

2 tablespoons apple cider vinegar

¼ teaspoon pepper

¼ teaspoon salt

¼ teaspoon dried dill weed, or ½ teaspoon fresh

Add the tomatoes, cucumbers, and onion to a serving bowl.

Season with the olive oil, apple cider vinegar, pepper, salt, and dill weed. Stir to coat all the ingredients evenly.

Refrigerate for 15 to 30 minutes before serving.

Fried Pork Chops

Deep-fried pork chops are a sought-after entrée in our family. My Dad and Walt both swear they will drive many a mile for a good pork chop. The bone-in pork chops offer so much more flavor than the boneless. Unlike pan-frying, which uses only enough oil to cover the bottom of a pan, deep-frying requires enough oil to cover the meat so that it floats in the oil while cooking, and creates a tasty crust around the entire pork chop.

Walt always serves Green Tabasco sauce alongside these fried pork chops to enhance the flavor. Give it a try!

Serves 6 to 8 --

1 quart vegetable oil
10 to 12 thin bone-in pork chops
2 tablespoons salt
2 tablespoons pepper
4 cups all-purpose flour
4 cups buttermilk

Pour enough oil into a deep-sided frying pan to cover the bottom about 2 inches. Heat the oil to 350 degrees F.

Salt and pepper the pork chops on both sides.

Pour the flour into a shallow dish.

Pour the buttermilk in a separate shallow dish.

Dredge the pork chops in the flour on both sides, then in the buttermilk, and again in the flour on both sides.

Once a chop is covered in batter, use a spatula to gently place the chop in the oil to fry. Do not crowd the pan. I usually cook 2 or 3 at a time in my large skillet.

Cook the pork chops 4 to 5 minutes on each side until golden brown. Use tongs to gently flip the pork chop when it looks golden brown, and cook the other side. The pork chop is done when a meat thermometer placed in the thickest part of the meat reads 145 degrees F.

Remove the pork chops to drain on a paper towel-covered plate. While you continue to fry the remaining pork chops, keep the cooked ones in a warm oven at 180 degrees F.

Summer Field Peas

Field peas are a delight of summer in the South, with wonderfully descriptive names like Purple Hull, Pink Eyes, Lady Peas, or—my favorite—White Acre Peas. You will find them in farmer's markets and fruit stands in late May and early June. I can remember both of my grandmothers shelling fresh peas when I was little. I liked to jump in and pop open a few, pulling the string out of the hull and pinching the mature peas out into a bowl. It's a time-consuming job, but the comaraderie around a table while shelling peas with family is always worth the effort. Nowadays you can find fresh peas with the hard work already done. But if you live next to a farmer, or know someone who hulls peas, ask to learn how it's done, then offer to help.

Serves 6 to 8

6 ounces salt pork, thinly sliced and cut in ½-inch slices, or you may substitute bacon slices
1 cup coarsely chopped onion
2 teaspoons chopped garlic
1 quart fresh field peas, rinsed
½ teaspoon salt
⅛ teaspoon pepper

In a soup pot or Dutch over, cook the pork over medium-high heat for 6 to 8 minutes to render the fat and brown the pork.

Once browned, reduce the heat to medium, add the onions, and cook 6 to 8 minutes until translucent and slightly brown on the edges. Once the onions begin to brown on the edges, add the garlic and cook for 1 to 2 minutes., until the garlic smells fragrant.

Add the peas to the pot along with 3 cups water, and the salt and pepper. Bring to a slow-rolling boil over medium-high heat, partially cover, then reduce the heat to medium and cook for 30 to 35 minutes until tender. Serve hot.

Squash Casserole

This is my Granny Cheney's recipe, with a few of my own adaptations. She knew it was my brother's and my favorite, so she made it often to show us how special we were to her. I make it every Thanksgiving and usually more than once in the summer. As a plus, you can prep these vegetables ahead of time. They will keep perfectly in a covered container in the refrigerator overnight.

Serves 8 to 10

3 tablespoons olive oil
7 cups yellow squash, roughly chopped
   into ½-inch pieces
1½ cups chopped onion
¾ teaspoon salt, divided
3 cups crumbled saltine crackers, divided
½ cup butter, melted
2 eggs, beaten
½ cup milk
3 cups grated cheddar cheese, divided
½ teaspoon pepper

Preheat the oven to 350 degrees F.

Heat the olive oil in a sauté pan over medium-high heat, and saute the squash for 5 minutes. Then add the chopped onion and ¼ teaspoon salt, and cook for 6 to 8 minutes, stirring often, until the squash is tender and the onions are translucent.

Pour the squash and onion mixture into a bowl.

In a separate bowl, stir 1½ cups of the saltine crumbles together with the melted butter. Mix well.

Add the other 1½ cups saltine crumbles to the squash and onion mixture, and stir well. To this mixture, stir in the eggs, milk, 1 cup grated cheese, the remaining ½ teaspoon salt, and the pepper until well combined.

Pour into a greased 9 x 13-inch baking dish. Sprinkle the remaining 2 cups grated cheese and the saltine and butter mixture over the top of the casserole. Bake for 45 minutes, or until light browned and bubbly.

Lemonade

Fresh cold lemonade is a welcomed treat on any Summer Day. Just like the sweet tea, you can garnish with fresh lemon slices and mint to make it even more special. Since some lemons are a little more tart than others, you may prefer to add extra simple syrup to your lemonade.

Serves 6 to 8

SIMPLE SYRUP
Yields approximately 3 cups

2 cups water
2 cups sugar

LEMONADE
1 cup fresh squeezed lemon juice
3 cups water
3 cups simple syrup

To make the Simple Syrup: Combine water and sugar in a saucpan over medium heat,and bring to a low and slow boil to dissolve the sugar into the water. Ready to use immediately.

To make the Lemonade: combine the lemon juice, water, and simple syrup in a pitcher. Stir together and serve over ice.

Cinnamon Ice Cream

When I was growing up in Savannah, we spent many special occasions—birthday meals, night out with friends and moms, dates, and now meals with my children—at Garibaldi's restaurant in City Market. They have my favorite dessert in town, the Berry Basket. There have been times when I knew they were getting close to running out, and we would ask the kitchen to save one for us. It is a caramel and sesame seed basket with ice cream, berries, and dark chocolate. Over the years, different ice creams have been included: vanilla, pistachio, and cinnamon. Cinnamon has long been my favorite ice cream, and it is my inspiration for this dessert.

If you are shopping for an ice cream maker, I recommend the Cuisinart 2-quart. It makes this and any ice cream easy to prepare, and it prepares the ice cream in 20 minutes (Resource Guide, p. 155).

Serves 8 -

2 cups whole milk
1 cup cream
½ cup sugar
1 teaspoon vanilla extract
1 teaspoon cinnamon

In medium bowl, whisk together the milk, cream, and sugar until the sugar dissolves.

Add the vanilla and cinnamon, and stir until well combined.

Pour in the ice cream maker and chill per instructions.

Serve with your choice of seasonal berry toppings.

Lonesome Dove Hunt BBQ

MENU

Boiled Peanuts

Bacon-Wrapped Doves

Tara's BBQ Sauce

Pulled Pork

Brunswick Stew

Potato Salad

Sweet Dill Pickles

Banana Pudding

As Walt would say, a good dove field is currency in our part of the world. For the hunters who have waited since turkey season in the spring to enjoy the opening of dove season on the first Saturday of September, the excitement is high. During the spring, dove hunters and farmers alike begin to prepare their coveted piece of land, and many hunters are excited to get back outdoors.

Wing shooting—the practice of shooting game birds in flight, including doves—is a social sport. I believe Walt loves this type of hunting the most, because he enjoys people so much. You have to have a good group of hunters shooting from blinds to keep the birds moving around the field, and keep the hunt going. It requires camaraderie and communication to enjoy a good shoot. If your field is flush with birds, most shooters worth their salt in shooting will limit. In Georgia the limit is usually 15 birds a day, per hunter.

I grew up with a brother that adored hunting, and a Dad that made sure Adam learned the art and appreciation of the woods. Then, I married into a family full of hunters. Actually, my first disagreement with Walt was over dove hunting. I wanted to go up to Athens for the UGA game on Labor Day weekend in 2005 (the year we started dating). Walt solemnly looked at me and quietly stated in no uncertain terms that he was going to be on a dove field the opening day of dove season. *Uh oh*. We worked it out. I went to the game, he went hunting, and then we met up afterwards. The first of many succesful compromises, I might add.

If you are the hunting sort, your preparation for this party begins about five months before the party starts. Cultivate your field with sunflowers, sorghum, or millet. As spring and summer ushers in fall, so your doves will come as well. We have had birds some years, and some years not. But either way, you can enjoy this menu anytime of the year that pleases you. My parents and the entire DeLoach family host this very party on July 4th every year. However, we prefer to host it Labor Day weekend, with the birds and hunters in attendance.

Many a BBQer would tell you that what I am about to write is sacrilege, but here goes. In my humble opinion, go ahead and cook your BBQ and Brunswick Stew a few days before so you don't have to stay up all night before the party. The Q and stew heat up just fine the day of the party, without causing you to sacrifice flavor.

Now, for all you hardcore BBQers, you can start your cooking 12 to 14 hours before that party if it makes you feel good. However, we prefer to hunt and throw a party all in the same day, and staying up all night doesn't fit into the schedule.

If you are the hunting sort, your preparation for this party begins about five months before the party starts. Cultivate your field with sunflowers, sorghum, or millet. As spring and summer ushers in fall, so your doves will come as well.

This is a great day to feed a crowd. You will have hungry hunters returning from the field and family members of the hunters gathering at the house. People will be coming and going, as limits are met on the field. People will eat in stages, and linger for hours as hunting stories are shared and enjoyed. I am sure your cousin will tell you he shot his limit of the dear peaceful dove, but in the end he could only find five. Of course, he said, the weeds on the field were too tall and thick, and he couldn't seem to find them to pick them up. Maybe so, maybe not, or maybe the dog ate the birds. As ole-timers do, we just let those stories grow year by year to enhance the day.

The Bar Table

It is a certainty in Southern get-togethers that guests will expect a table of alcoholic libations for their refreshment. After our big dove hunts, we often offer up a bar so friends can readily help themselves. It's usually set indoors, or on a porch away from the food table, so that it's easy to congregate around. This allows hosts to point guests in the direction of the bar to help themselves, while we keep the party moving along elsewhere. Serve the wine and beer in a cold bucket, and arrange bottles of any liquor of your choice. However, Southern bar tables will always include an excellent choice of whiskey and bourbon. Whatever guests prefer—neat, on the rocks, wine, beer, or a mixed drink—a party is judged not only by the food, but by the quality of the bar.

This is a great day to feed a crowd. You will have hungry hunters returning from the field and family members of the hunters gathering at the house. People will be coming and going, as limits are met on the field. People will eat in stages, and linger for hours as hunting stories are shared and enjoyed.

Boiled Peanuts

Affectionally known as the "caviar of the South," boiled peanuts are a roadside staple here in Georgia. Whether headed to the beach or to a football game, boiled peanuts are one of our favorite snacks. My Aunt Susan would always boil a batch for us when we would go to visit them in St. Augustine in the summer. Now, I do the very same for my family when we go to the beach, and we always enjoy them as a tasty treat during dove season.

Green peanuts are availble in the mid-summer to late fall months, and can be found at many farmers markets in the South. You can also order them from Hardy Farms in Hawkinsville, Georgia (Resource Guide, p. 155). In Georgia you often find these wet delicacies served up in plastic–lined paper bags or styrofoam cups.

Be careful not to over–salt them. When they soak for the last 30 minutes, much of the salt is absorbed. If you think your are a little too salty, you can pour out the original brine and add fresh water to the peanuts for a brief soak to reduce the salty taste. Boiled Peanuts go down great with cold beer, and don't be afraid to throw the shells on the ground if you're eating outdoors at my house!

Yields 2 pounds peanuts --

2 pounds green peanuts
¼ cup salt

Add the peanuts and salt to to a stockpot filled with 5 quarts water, partially cover, and bring to a boil over high heat, then lower the heat to a medium rolling boil and cook for 3 hours.

After 3 hours, cover with a tight-fitting lid, remove from the heat, and let the peanuts soak at room temperature for 30 minutes, then drain the water and serve immediately.

They will keep in the refrigerator for 3 days, and are delicious enjoyed cold.

Bacon-Wrapped Doves

In our part of the world, doves are available during dove season, which starts in September and goes through early winter. If you aren't a hunter, this wild game will most often be available for you to cook if you call your dove hunting buddy, and ask him to help you hunt some birds. Alternatively, hunters will freeze the doves so the meat can be thawed and enjoyed after the dove season has ended. This recipe can be doubled or tripled, of course.

Serves 4 to 6

12 dove breasts, deboned
3 strips of bacon, cut in half
1½ cups Dale's seasoning
½ teaspoon pepper

Preheat your grill to 350 degrees F.

Wrap 2 dove breasts in ½ of a bacon strip. Secure the bacon and dove breasts with a wooden skewer. Continue until all the breasts are wrapped and secured.

Pour the Dale's Seasoning into a bowl and add the doves. Soak the dove breasts for 10 minutes.

After 10 minutes, remove the dove breasts and lightly sprinkle with pepper.

Grill the bacon-wrapped doves for 10 minutes, turning after 5 minutes. You will want the doves breasts to be medium-rare when finished and ready to eat.

Tara's BBQ Sauce

This is a vinegar-based sauce. It is tasty on pork or chicken, and keeps well in the refrigerator.

Yields approximately 4½ cups --

3 cups apple cider vinegar
1½ cup ketchup
2 tablespoons Worcestershire sauce
4 tablespoons brown sugar
1 tablespoon orange juice
1 teaspoon pepper
1 teaspoon garlic granules
½ teaspoon dried minced onion
¼ teaspoon red pepper
¼ teaspoon cayenne pepper

Whisk all ingredients together in a saucepan over medium-high heat for 10 minutes, stirring often.

Once mixed well, you can refrigerate it in a lidded container for 3 to 5 days, or heat and use it immediately. It can also be reheated.

Pork Dry Rub

When I was first married and trying to navigate my way around the kitchen, My Granny is the one who told me about adding cinnamon to roasted pork. This pork roast was one of the first dishes I made. Try it! I guarantee you'll like it.

Yields about ½ cup rub --

4 tablespoons kosher salt
4 teaspoons pepper
4 teaspoons garlic powder
3 teaspoons cinnamon

Mix all ingredients together in a small bowl, and pat onto the pork on all sides.

Use on pork for roasting, as well as on pork for your grill or smoker.

Pulled Pork

Serves 10 to 12

1 (7 to 8-pound) bone-in Boston Butt
(pork shoulder)
7 to 8 tablespoons of Dry Rub for
pork (recipe, p. 97)

Preheat the oven or smoker to 250 degrees F.

Rub the Boston Butt liberally with the pork rub. Place the pork in the roaster or smoker with the fatty side up.

Cook 12 to 14 hours, or until a meat thermometer inserted in the thickest part of the meat reads 195 degrees F.

Cover with foil, and let the meat rest for 30 minutes before pulling the meat.

How to Pull Pork

Use two forks to pull the meat from the bone, shredding it as you pull. Discard the bone, and continue to shred all the meat. Keep those burnt ends intact, they're tasty!

Brunswick Stew

The base of Brunswick Stew is chicken stock. Many people think that it is a pork stew, and it often is. However, it can include any meat you prefer. I made a batch for a friend using only chicken, and it was delicious. Historically people would add squirrel, rabbit, or any meat they had on hand. My grandparents used ground beef pushed through a grinder for their recipe. That fascinated me as a child!

It will scorch in a hot minute, so you must stand right over the pot when you cook, stirring constantly. Also, it tastes better the second day after being in the refrigerator. But you absolutely MUST reheat it slowly, or it will burn and the whole stew will be ruined!

Serves 12 to 14

BOILED CHICKEN STOCK
Yields approximately 3 quarts stock

1 (3 to 5-pound) chicken, bone-in, skin on, cut in pieces
2 tablespoons kosher salt
1 tablespoon pepper
3 onions, coarsely chopped

STEW
3 quarts boiled chicken stock
5 cups shredded chicken
3 cups pulled pork
2 cups Tara's BBQ sauce (recipe, p. 97)
2 (28-ounce) cans crushed tomatoes
4 (14.75 ounce) cans lima beans, drained
4 (14.75 ounce) cans white creamed corn
4 bay leaves
3 tablespoons Worcestershire sauce
½ teaspoon dried minced garlic
2 tablespoons brown sugar
8 tablespoons butter

To make the Stock: Salt and pepper a whole chicken and place it in a stockpot. Add the chopped onions and 3 quarts water to cover.

Boil the chicken on medium-high to high, partially covered, for about 20 minutes, until fully cooked. It is ready when the meat falls easily from the bone. Once fully cooked, remove the chicken and all bones from the stock. Debone the cooked chicken, and discard the bones. Shred the chicken by pulling it apart with two forks. Return it to the stock.

To make the Brunswick Stew: Combine all ingredients in the pot with the stock. Bring to a simmer over medium-high heat, stirring constantly. Reduce the heat to medium-low, and cook for 30 to 45 minutes, stirring often. The stew is done when the lima beans are soft and tender.

Remember to remove the bay leaves before serving.

Potato Salad

This is my version of my Aunt Pam Huff's recipe. She serves it at most every family gathering. I recommend Yukon gold potatoes. You can leave the ¼ teaspoon cayenne pepper out, depending on how hot you want it. The kick it adds is not too hot, and really llifts the traditional flavors. In our family, we serve this warm, and it's divine. Of course, it can be refrigerated. And you can reheat it in the microwave.

Be careful not to add too much mayo if you think it's dry. It's easier to add than take away. And I always use Duke's mayo—it's the best.

Serves 8 to 10 --

8 cups potatoes, peeled and cut into
   ½-inch cubes
3 teaspoons salt
½ cup dill pickle juice
1 teaspoon garlic powder
¼ teaspoon salt
¼ teaspoon pepper
⅛ teaspoon cayenne pepper (optional)
3 tablespoons Dijon mustard
½ cup Duke's mayonnaise
8 dill spears, coarsely chopped

Add 5 cups water, the potato cubes, and salt to a large pot over high heat. Boil 8 to 10 minutes until fork tender.

Drain the water, leaving only the piping hot potatoes in the pot. Pour in the dill pickle juice.

Sprinkle the potatoes with garlic powder, salt, pepper and cayenne pepper, and stir to combine.

Next add the Dijon mustard, mayo, and pickles, and mix thoroughly.

May be served warm or cold.

Sweet Dill Pickles

These pickles are delicious and so easy to make! It is a family favorite of Walt's sisters. The original version comes from their grandmother, Mable Jones Coleman, of Camak, Georgia. It can be doubled, or even quadrupled to make a gallon. I think my interpretation at 32 ounces is perfect to keep in the fridge, or to give as a hostess gift. These keep getting tastier in the refrigerator the longer they sit. And you can use more or less garlic, according to your liking. You'll find these pickles will quickly disappear. In fact, this jar was full when we started shooting!

Yields 32 ounces

32 ounces dill pickle chips, your favorite
   brand, divided
2 cups sugar, divided
2 cloves garlic, peeled, thinly sliced,
   and divided

Empty the storebought jar of pickles along with the syrup into a bowl. Drain the syrup and discard.

Using the original pickle jar, or a lidded jar of your choosing, and layer the ingredients accordingly: ½ cup sugar, ¼ garlic slices, 1 cup pickle chips.

Repeat the layers until the jar is full and the ingredients are all used. Place the lid back on the jar and roll the jar around on your counter to mix the ingredients.

Refrigerate for at least 6 hours before serving. The sugar will dissolve and pull moisture from the pickles, keeping them moist and tasty. In fact, they taste better the longer they are in your refrigerator.

Banana Pudding

This is always a crowd pleaser. It is my version of my Aunt Patty's recipe. She makes it for Walt at all of our family get-togethers. For a traditional dessert, this one can't be beat. The cream cheese makes it rich and the Cool Whip keeps it light. So good!

Serves 12

1 (3.4 ounce) packet Jell-O vanilla pudding
1 (3.4 ounce) packet Jell-O banana cream
   pudding
3 cups cold milk
8 ounces cream cheese, at room temperature
1 (14-ounce) can condensed milk
2 cups Cool Whip
8 bananas, sliced ¼-inch thick
2 (11-ounce) boxes Vanilla Wafers, divided

In a large mixing bowl, combine both packages of puddings with 3 cups of milk and let them set according to package directions.

In a mixer, whip the cream cheese and the condensed milk until well combined.

Add this mixture to the pudding bowl.

Fold in the Cool Whip in until well combined.

To layer, use a large trifle dish (like this one in the photo), or a large flat-bottomed bowl. Begin with whole Vanilla Wafers to cover the bottom of the bowl, then add sliced bananas, and then cover with the pudding/Cool Whip mixture. Repeat this process two more times, ending with the pudding mixture on top.

If you use a clear glass bowl, you can "church it up" by placing vanilla wafers facing out at each layer, as shown.

Top with a handful of crumbled Vanilla Wafers.

Après Funeral

A Potluck Party in Their Honor and Their Absence

When I was in college at UGA, I tried in earnest to figure out what I should be when I graduated. So, my junior year I marched down to the College and Career Advising Center to take a personality test that would match me with my perfect job. I completed the hour-or-so test and out came my suggested careers. Career Suggestion #1: Funeral Director. *Not lying to you!* FUNERAL DIRECTOR. Now, I am not saying this to offend those that work in such a respectable occupation. It's just, at 21 years of age, does funeral director come to mind as the thing you really want to do? Not to me. I just laughed at that list, and walked out. My first job after college was as a merchandise girl in Colorado for a local Athens band. I traveled with the band selling CD's, scullies, and t-shirts with their logo on it, from a booth in the back. Basically, I saw Colorado from the inside of a bar. Fun, but let's save that story for the next collection of recipes.

Fast Forward twenty-one years since I took that test, and I will admit that I would be a fantastic funeral director. That test was spot on. I have learned through experience what important attributes it takes to give a family a supportive and heartfelt funeral experience. I have learned this because I have had the honor of helping organize the obituaries, details, and logistics of funerals for some people dearest to my heart. All my party-planning skills absolutely have a place in planning a successful celebration of the people we lose.

All the celebration, tradition, and comfort shared over the casseroles of our past are sure to hold a special place in the hearts of those most needing

MENU

Fried Chicken

———

Macaroni and Cheese

———

Broccoli Casserole

———

Deviled Eggs

———

Pound Cake

———

comfort. And what better way to show love than to feed people?

Whether there is a funeral, memorial service, interment, or simply ashes in an urn, at some point at the end of the day mourners will gather at a house, usually the home of the spouse or the closest living relative in the town. It is here where the heaviness of the day is carried on the shoulders of those sitting next to you. It is where high heels are traded for slippers, play clothes are put on children, and the porches, couches, and bottom steps of stairs are filled with those in mourning.

Ironically, some of my fondest memories of connection are shared in these precious moments. It is a sacred time. There is a sense of knowing amongst those at this gathering. All are welcome, and those that choose to share in this party know that they are either the ones being cared for, or the ones taking care of those who are most grieved.

When someone passes away in the South, an army of church ladies and dear friends begin to organize THE FOOD. I capitalize "the food" because it's a critical element of a successful funeral. Food is a main character in the story of grief. You will probably find a dozen pound cakes on the counter of the bereaved family before the sun goes down on the day of the loved one's passing. There are ladies that organize who will bring

the ham and the platter of cold cuts to make sandwiches, the potato salad, the macaroni salad, the tea, and the plates, forks, napkins, and spoons. All of this food is to be assembled at the home immediately as the news moves through town. There will be a guestbook where those who come to pay their respects at the home of the bereaved will sign their name before dropping off their home-baked goodness. Each Southern cook knows they have a family favorite they must share at times of sadness. I rely heavily on pound cakes and breakfast goodies for the morning of the funeral.

As you can imagine, my grandmother DeLoach is one of these ladies. Often, groups of friends and colleagues will organize the food for the bereaved the week before the funeral. While my grandmother was a middle school principal, a husband of one of the teachers passed away. As the principal, Grandmother organized the other teachers to bring a covered dish to be served at the luncheon at the home of the bereaved after the interment.

The day of the funeral, Grandmother gathered up the food in coolers at her school, and took it to the home of her teacher while the funeral was still going on. She had been instructed that the front door to the house would be open, and to go right in. So she did. She walked into the kitchen and prepared to set out the food, so that when the close friends and family arrived lunch would immediately be served. As she looked around, she noticed the house had not been picked up, and certainly didn't have the look of cleanliness and order one would expect with guests arriving. So, before setting out the food, she decided it would be in the best interest to clean up the kitchen and gathering area before everyone returned.

Finally, after cleaning, drying, and putting away the dishes and tidying up, it was time to set out the prepared lunch. At this time, it dawned on Grandmother that maybe something was amiss. Why wasn't this kitchen already cleaned? She decided to walk outside and check the address just to be sure. Across the street, a neighbor was standing in the yard looking at her oddly.

"They aren't home," Grandmother announced in explanation. "They are at the funeral home, as they have lost their mother."

The neighbor shook his head and said, "No one has lost anyone at that home. It's this family at… " and he pointed to one house over. Sure enough, she was at the wrong house! Horrified, Grandmother quickly ran inside the neighbor's home, packed up the lunch, took it over to the already neat and tidy home of the bereaved, and set everything out in readiness. After correcting her mistake, she hurried on her way to teach a scheduled class to school administrators, as she was late from cleaning and putting out lunch twice.

When she arrived, she announced to the class of aspiring educators, "If you see a policeman, he is here for me. I am in big trouble because I broke into someone's home." Oh, she was so upset. Still is! She later called the woman who had lost her mother, and explained the story. She assured Grandmother that she would let her neighbors know, and to not think a thing of it. Of course the other homeowners were most gracious and never pressed charges. Who would, if they had come home to a clean house?

Southern food sustains our souls in celebrations

When someone passes away in the South, an army of church ladies and dear friends begin to organize THE FOOD. I capitalize "the food" because it's a critical element of a successful funeral.

throughout our lives, and helps give us strength as we usher our loved ones into the heavenly hereafter. The funeral party is there to create warmth, lift a heavy burden, and offer rest to the weary family, while guests enjoy a bounty of pound cake.

One piece of advice: if your funeral takes place in the fall, you might want to move that funeral to Friday or Sunday afternoon, should Saturday be suggested. There are just some folks on the other side not interested in interrupting peoples' game days. To our children, please count me in on that one. I am sure your father would agree.

In much of the South, you can count on many of the dishes featured in this chapter to show up on the table. However, please remember this party is a community effort. An army of people will bring items. I guarantee that the first to show up will be the pound cakes and cold cuts with iced tea. Since you don't know what others are bringing, make sure that you bring what is needed to best enjoy your dish. Afterward, I suggest you leave your leftover contributions in a pretty disposable dish with nice-looking disposable serving pieces that will help the family in cleaning up. However, should you leave a non-disposable dish, remember to put your name on the bottom with piece of paper covered in tape, so they will know who to return it to in the coming days.

Fried Chicken

Oh, what a fine delicacy of the South! Fried chicken is an execution of simple ingredients done well. This is Walt's favorite food, and his mother sure knows how best to cook it—this is her recipe. The brine is key to the taste. She also said to be sure to puncture the liver before frying, or it will splatter and burn. You can tuck the chicken wing under itself to fry. Be sure to check for doneness, as the dark meat will take longer to cook than the light meat.

Serves 8

2 (3-pound) fryer chickens, cut up,
   with parts, no necks
3 tablespoons salt, for the brine
1½ cups self-rising flour
2 teaspoons pepper, divided
1½ teaspoons salt, divided
2 quarts vegetable oil, for frying

In a large bowl, add 4 cups hot water and the salt. Add the cut-up chicken pieces and parts, making sure the brine covers them. Cover the bowl and let the chicken brine for 2 hours at room temperature.

After 2 hours, remove from the water and drain the chicken pieces on a paper towel. Pat them dry.

Arrange the chicken on 2 cookie sheets.

To prepare the seasoned flour, pour the flour into a deep pan. Add 1 teaspoon pepper and 1 teaspoon salt, and mix well.

With the remaining salt and pepper, season the chicken pieces evenly on all sides.

Next, roll the chicken pieces in the seasoned flour mixture, filling the creases of each piece with a spoon to cover thoroughly. Lay the floured chicken on the cookie sheets; do not stack them.

Fill an 8-quart pot with the vegetable oil and heat to 325 degrees F.

Using long tongs, place the chicken into the hot oil, one piece at a time. Be sure not to overcrowd the pot.

The wings will take nearly 12 minutes to cook, the breasts nearly 15 minutes, and the dark meat closer to 20 minutes.

Remove each piece as it is fully cooked, and drain on a paper-towel-lined platter for at least 5 minutes before serving.

Macaroni and Cheese

This is my Granny Cheney's most famous recipe. It fills a 9 x 13-inch casserole dish, or a deep round baking dish such as the one shown. Using a deep dish prevents dripping. And be sure to let the pasta mixture rest for the full 10 minutes, per the recipe below. This is a very important step. You will want the casserole to be very soupy when you put it in the oven. If you need extra moisture, stir in ½ cup of pasta water or milk, or as much as needed before baking. And remember, always grate your own cheese! It melts so much more evenly, and has more moisture.

Serves 12

2 tablespoons, plus 1 teaspoon salt
1 (16-ounce) box ziti
2 cups grated extra sharp cheddar, divided
2 cups grated Colby cheddar, divided
2 eggs beaten
½ cup milk
3 tablespoons Duke's mayonnaise
¾ cup butter (12 tablespoons)
2 tablespoons sugar
4 tablespoons sour cream
¼ teaspoon pepper

Preheat the oven to 350 degrees F.

Fill a large pot with 4 quarts of water and add 2 tablespoons of salt. Bring to a boil over high heat, and cook the ziti until it is just past al dente. Drain most of the pasta, saving 2 cups of the pasta water. Keep the cooked pasta warm in the pot.

Beat the eggs in a small bowl. Add the milk and beat to combine.

To the warm pasta pot, add 1 cup of each cheese, the beaten eggs and milk, mayo, butter, sugar, sour cream, 1 teaspoon salt, and the pepper. Stir until the cheese and butter have melted a bit, then pour the mixture into a greased baking dish, and let it sit at room temperature for 10 minutes.

The ingredients should still be soupy after 10 minutes. If needed, add the remaining pasta water in ½ cup increments to achieve the desired moisture. Then cover the top with the remaining 2 cups of cheese.

Bake for 50 to 55 minutes. When the sides of the macaroni and cheese begin to bubble and brown, the casserole is ready.

Broccoli Casserole

This is my adaptation of my good friend Sandy Dillard's recipe. It's delicious! She recommends smashing and breaking the broccoli up with a fork before mixing. I serve it in an 8 x 8-inch casserole dish.

Serves 4 to 8

1 (32-ounce) package frozen broccoli
3 cups grated cheese, divided
1 (10.5-ounce) can cream of
   mushroom soup
2 eggs, beaten
¾ cup Duke's mayonnaise
¼ teaspoon salt
1 cup crumbled Ritz Crackers
¼ cup melted butter

Preheat the oven to 350 degrees F.

Cook the broccoli according to package directions, and set aside. When it has cooled enough, use a fork to smash and break up the broccoli into bite-size bits.

In a large mixing bowl, stir together the broccoli, mushroom soup, eggs, mayo, salt, and 1 cup of cheese.

Pour into the casserole dish, and top with the remaining 2 cups of cheese. Cover with the crumbled Ritz Crackers, and pour the melted butter on top of the crumbles.

Cook for 45 minutes, or until the casserole is golden and bubbly.

Deviled Eggs

My Uncle Lou Cason is a legend when it comes to making these Deviled Eggs. He suggests the key to success is in mixing the dry ingredients with the yolks before adding any mayonnaise. I agree!

Yields 24 halves

12 boiled eggs
½ teaspoon ground mustard
¼ teaspoon garlic powder
⅛ teaspoon white pepper
¼ teaspoon of salt
½ cup Duke's mayonnaise
3 tablespoons Mt. Olive sweet salad cubes, or substitute pickle relish
6 gherkin pickles, sliced in thirds on the slant

Peel the boiled eggs, cut in half the long way (as shown in the photo), and separate the cooked egg yolks from the whites.

Put the egg yolks in one bowl, and the egg whites on a plate, or a deviled egg platter.

In the egg yolk bowl, stir together the ground mustard, garlic powder, white pepper, and salt until well combined. Add the Duke's mayo and pickles into the egg yolk mixture and stir to combine.

Spoon the mixture into the egg white halves. Garnish with a slice of a gherkin pickle. Serve immediately, or refrigerate before serving.

How To Boil Eggs

Place 12 raw eggs in a pot with enough water to cover the eggs by at least ½-inch. Bring the eggs to a boil on high heat.

Once boiling, turn off the heat and cover the pot. Let stand for 11 minutes for a perfectly hard-boiled egg (don't ask me why, but this is what works).

After 11 minutes, drain and rinse the eggs under cold water to stop the cooking. Let them cool for 2 to 3 minutes more, then peel and enjoy!

Pound Cake

There will assuredly be many delivered, but go ahead and prepare at least one cake for the party. This is my mother-in-law Rebecca Rocker's recipe that she received and adapted from Mrs. Edith Brock of Eatonton, Georgia. It is a good idea to pull your eggs and butter out of the refrigerator ahead of time to let them come to room temperature before using. Also, my mother always suggested this—and she is always right: Crack each egg individually in its own bowl before adding it to the recipe. That way, if you have a bad egg it will not ruin the bunch. Also, traditionally, we flavor our pound cake with vanilla extract. You can choose your preference. However, my mother-in law swears by butternut flavoring if you can find it. She orders hers from Amazon (Resource Guide, p. 155).

Serves 12 to 14

1 cup butter, room temperature
3 cups sugar
6 eggs, separated, whites and yolks
    saved separately
¼ teaspoon baking soda
1 cup sour cream
pinch of salt
3 cups all-purpose flour
1 teaspoon vanilla extract

Optional: in place of vanilla extract,
you may use 1 teaspoon of either
lemon or orange extract, or butternut
flavoring

Preheat the oven to 300 degrees F.

Cream the butter and sugar in the bowl of a mixer.

Separate the eggs. Save the whites and set aside. Add the yolks to the creamed butter and sugar, mixing well. Let this sit in the mixer until you combine the next ingredients.

In a bowl, stir the baking soda into the sour cream until it dissolves.

In a separate bowl, sift together the salt and the flour.

In the mixer, on low speed, add some of the flour mixture, then some of the sour cream to the ingredients in the mixer, alternating additions, and beginning and ending with flour.

Add the vanilla extract, or your choice of flavorings, and continue to mix on medium to low speed.

Beat the saved egg whites in a bowl using a handheld mixer until stiff peaks form.

Fold the egg whites into the batter in the mixer, being careful not to over mix.

Grease and flour a stem pan or Bundt pan.

Pour the batter in the pan. Lightly drop the pan on the counter a couple of times to help the batter settle.

Bake for 1 hour and 20 minutes on the middle rack.

Set the pan aside to cool for at least 30 minutes before removing the cake from the pan.

Hearty Halloween
Soup Cauldrons

Anne, the beloved character of one of my favorite children's books, *Anne of Green Gables*, used exactly the right words when she said, "I'm so glad I live in a world where there are Octobers." I am too. October ushers in crisp fall mornings, bidding adieu to the sweaty, swampy Indian summer of the South that seems to linger forever. Also, it is the birthday month of some of my favorite people, including Walt, his dad, and our son, Ford. We start a steady march of celebrations in the fall that culminate on New Year's day.

Halloween is one of the highlights of the season, of course, and the neighborhood children, including our own, especially enjoy this scare-fest. Halloween is the biggest night out for neighbors in our small town of 6,000. Since we live in a rural community, those that live on a family farm, or just a bit outside the city limits, also come to town to trick-or-treat. When you add in the neighbors from far and wide, I estimate that about 2,000 or so ghosts and goblins march up and down our street that evening.

Hosting a big party for the parents and kids is traditional in our neighborhood. Walt absolutely loves this party, too. The only rule we have (and he put it in place, not me) is that all attendees are required to dress up. In years past we have seen adult friends portray the characters from "The Big Lebowski," and this year we are hosting "A Christmas

MENU

Baguette Toast

French Onion Soup

---

*Italian Sausage and
Mushroom Soup*

Halloween Haystacks

Halloween night in our little town recalls old-timey movies of American neighborhoods in the mid-Twentieth Century. Children running down the street, doors wide open, friends on the porch, candlelit pumpkins, costume parties, and a warm cup or bowl of soup.

Vacation" for Halloween. Everyone brings a bag of candy, an appetizer, or a dessert, and we have a ball handing out the candy and watching our kiddos run through the neighborhood. It looks like the Halloween scene straight out of ET.

I will have to admit, I am more of the "friendly-ghost" Halloween type, as I admit to still being a little afraid of the dark. When the Netflix thriller *Stranger Things* came out, my brother Adam told me, "Tara you have to watch this! It's all about when we were kids! It's full of 80's stuff!" Well, that was intriguing, but I knew it was scary, so I wasn't sure I could handle the thrill of it all. Nevertheless, curiosity prevailed, and Walt and I were immediately hooked. I had to watch the entire first season with my hand partially covering one eye!

Not to release any spoilers, but I will tell you there is a monster called the "Demogorgon." Terrible, frightening thing! One night, after a particularly scary episode, I couldn't sleep. I lay awake thinking about the survival of our children in the face of such an evil creature lurking in the shadows. Walt was sound asleep next to me, while my eyes were wide open.

"W-a-l-t" I whispered in hushed tones. "Walt, are you awake?"

"No, I'm asleep," he replied.

Whew, he was awake, thank goodness. "Walt, do you think the children are breathing?" I asked.

"Yes, Tara."

Still worried, I asked, "Are you sure? Do you think you could go upstairs and just look, you know, just look at them for me?" Silence. More Silence.

Then he said, "You go, you're awake."

Frozen, I lay there still and quiet. Finally I confessed, "I... I'm too scared, Walt." He didn't move or open his eyes. Then he spoke the truth of it in the darkness of that night. He said, "You're afraid the Demogorgon is going to get you and the kids, aren't you?"

Yes! Yes, exactly! I thought to myself. He knows me well. But to try and save face I squeaked out, "Maybe… ?"

Quietly, he lay there, and then stated, "I am going to do this once, and once only. This is the last time I go looking for the Demogorgon."

Oh, sweet relief! Walt slowly marched upstairs, looked at our children, and made sure they were still breathing. They were! Thankfully the creatures under the bed weren't bothering anyone that night, just my imagination.

The main dish of our Halloween evening is Walt's Soup. As I said before, my man can cook. And his soups speak for themselves. They are rich with depth and flavor. And of course the temperature of Halloween night usually welcomes a warm pot of soup, while leaving a little room for the treats. He begins the cooking process a few days in advance, to be sure all the flavors get to know each other before mealtime. Each year he prepares French onion soup in one pot—excuse

me, cauldron—and sausage and mushroom soup in the other. We serve the soup in paper bowls, to keep things casual, and so kids can sit anywhere in the yard, house, or porch and eat anytime during the spookery. It's a delicious evening!

Halloween night in our little town recalls old-timey movies of American neighborhoods in the mid-Twentieth Century—children running down the street, doors wide open, friends on the porch, candle-lit pumpkins, costume parties, and a warm cup or bowl of soup.

Our three children are growing before our eyes—our oldest is a teenager. I know they won't be here for Halloween forever, and the loss of these days pulls at my heartstrings.

How fleeting are the days of childhood! I'm certain, though, that the fun of our small town Halloween nights will live on in their memories… and maybe even on their stoves.

Baguette Toast

Yields 8 to 16 slices --

1 baguette, sliced
3 to 4 tablespoons olive oil
3 cloves garlic, peeled

Heat the oven to broil.

Slice the baguette into ½-inch pieces. Place on a cookie sheet, and brush each side of the bread with olive oil.

Broil each side for 1 minute, turning, or until golden brown. Before serving, rub the peeled garlic across the top of the toast to give it a hint of garlic.

French Onion Soup

This is my version of a family favorite. French Onion soup is one of my favorite meals to cook. It takes time, as you have to let the onions cook down slowly. Do your best not to rush that step. It makes for a glorious finale! Note: Be sure your soup bowls are oven friendly before melting the cheese on broil.

Serves 6 to 8

20 cups sliced yellow onions
5 tablespoons olive oil
2½ teaspoons salt
3 teaspoons all-purpose flour
3 cloves garlic, finely chopped
2 quarts Kitchen Basics Beef Stock Salted
6 sprigs thyme
3 sprigs rosemary
¼ teaspoon pepper
8 to 16 pieces baguette toast (recipe, p. 126)
3 cups shredded gruyere cheese

Place the sliced onions in a large stockpot with the olive oil. Sprinkle with salt, stir to coat the slices, and cook down over medium heat for approximately 1 hour, stirring often and scraping the bottom of the pot. The onions will begin to turn brown as they caramelize and the water cooks out of them.

Once the onions have cooked down, add the flour and cook for 3 minutes, stirring constantly. Then add the chopped garlic. Cook for 2 minutes, stirring constantly. Add the beef stock.

Roll the herbs in a cheesecloth and tie with twine. Place the herbs in the soup, increase the heat to high and bring to a boil. Immediately lower the heat to medium-low and simmer for 30 minutes.

Once the soup has finished simmering, turn the broiler on. Ladle the soup into oven-friendly bowls.

Place one or two pieces of baguette toast atop the soup.

Top each bowl with 2 to 3 tablespoons of shredded gruyere cheese.

Place the bowls on a cookie sheet and put them in the broiler for 1 to 2 minutes to melt the cheese. The cheese should be melted and bubbly when ready. Serve immediately.

Italian Sausage and Mushroom Soup

Like any good soup, making it early allows the flavors to "get to know each other," as my mother often says. So, make this a day or two ahead, if possible.

Serves 12, can be halved

2 to 3 pounds Italian Sausage,
    sliced into bite-size coins
4 cups sliced fresh button mushrooms
2 cups thinly sliced onions
1 teaspoon salt, divided
2 tablespoons olive oil
2 tablespoons minced garlic
2½ quarts salted beef stock
Salt and pepper to taste

Heat a large stockpot or Dutch oven over medium-high heat. Add the sausage and cook, stirring often, for 10 minutes, or until the sausage has browned and cooked through.

Using a slotted spoon, spoon the sausage out into a separate bowl, leaving the drippings in the pot.

In the same pot over medium-high heat, add the sliced mushrooms, ½ teaspoon salt, and the olive oil. (The key is to get the moisture out of the mushrooms to enhance the flavor.) Cook them for 10 minutes, stirring often, then add the sliced onions and the remaining ½ teaspoon salt.

The onion-mushroom mixture will need to cook on medium heat for 15 minutes, stirring often to cook evenly. Once the onions and mushroom begin to brown at the edges, add the garlic and cook for 2 minutes.

Add the sausage back into the pot along with the beef stock. Mix well so all ingredients are well incorporated, and cooking evenly.

Reduce the heat to low so it is just bubbling, and simmer, paritally covered, for 45 minutes. The soup is done when the sausage is fork tender and cooked through.

Halloween Haystacks

This is the best recipe for children to make themselves on Halloween! They can showcase their talents in the kitchen, and let friends and family know they made it all by themselves. Our daughters love to make this treat. Especially Eleanor, the youngest. The candy can be melted on the stovetop with the help of an adult, or in the microwave. Be sure to lick the spoon!

Makes 2 dozen

11 ounces butterscotch morsels
12 ounces chow mein noodles
3 ounces dark chocolate morsels

Melt the butterscotch morsels in a large microwave-safe bowl on medium-high for 2 minutes. Stir the morsels to be sure they are thoroughly melted.

Pour the noodles into the butterscotch mixture. Stir well until all the butterscotch is used, and the noodles are completely covered.

Cover a cookie sheet with wax paper.

Use your fingers, or a serving spoon, to scoop out the butterscotch-covered noodles, and form them into individual haystacks. Place them on the cookie sheet.

Once the haystacks are formed, melt the chocolate in a bowl in the microwave on medium-high for 1 to 2 minutes, checking after 1 minute. Once melted thoroughly, dip a fork into the chocolate, and use the fork to drizzle chocolate on top of the haystacks. Place the pan in the freezer, uncovered, for 10 minutes to speed up the cooling process, and serve when they are firm. If you prefer, use a metal spatula to transfer them to a serving plate.

They can be kept in an airtight container at room temperature for 3 to 5 days.

The Life-Changing Oyster Roast

I was offered my first real job at an oyster roast, and that job changed my life.

Let me explain.

I attended Savannah Country Day School from seventh through twelfth grade. What a place! I love it to this day. They do a great job of keeping their alumni engaged. One of the events, usually held around Thanksgiving, is an alumni oyster roast. In 2002, I was home from college for the holiday and decided to attend. I figured that oyster roasts are great places to meet friends that you haven't seen in a while. In what is usually the first cool spell of the season, everyone stands around a table, shucking oysters, talking, and catching up.

As I walked up to the first table of oysters, I spotted our beloved headmaster, Dr. Paul Pressley. In school, he always spoke to us in a personable way. He was, and is, a gracious man. For example, during my senior year a few of us upper-school cheerleaders were being obnoxious before a home game. We had driven over to the local convenience store for snacks, and decided it would be a good idea to yell obscenities to one another from our cars. I was driving a group, and my good friend was driving the other car. Well, of course, a grown-up caught us.

MENU

Roasted Oysters

Andouille Chili

Sweet Jalapeño Cornbread Muffins

Lemon Layers

She let the school know that our behavior was a very poor representation of the kind of students and people that Country Day was shaping. After the phone call, Dr. Pressly pulled each one of us into his office for a talk. I was scared, but he was stern, honest, and let me know just how disappointed he was that I would set such a bad example in the community. I looked down at my penny loafers in shame. And that was it. He said good luck cheering tonight, and don't let anything like this happen again. Grace was shared.

So, naturally I was excited to talk to him again. I went on and on about graduating from UGA in December as I just needed one more football season. (I know you fans understand.) He looked at me and said, "Tara, would you like a ticket to anywhere in this country to go and talk to alumni about Country Day? Be a 'road warrior' of sorts?"

I was surprised, but immediately said, "Sure! Sounds like fun! I would love that." So, it was settled. I began conversations with the development director at the time, John Reddan (who has become one of my favorite people), and I started working the following February 2003.

Oyster Roasts are always held outdoors, as they are messy. They are especially popular in months that end in "-ER," somewhat popular in months ending in one "R." Really, fall and winter are the best and most popular times to hold a roast.

Most oyster-eaters will consume 1 or 2 dozen oysters at an oyster roast. You can roast them in a variety of ways. Traditionally, a fire pit is lit, a metal sheet is placed over the pit, and oysters are poured onto the metal sheet to cook over the open fire. We moisten burlap sacks with water, and use them to cover the oysters, which steams them as they cook. Watch the oysters to see when the shells pop open, indicating they are finished roasting.

Alternatively, you can steam the oysters in a pot with a slotted strainer. Place a brick in a large pot, fill it with a little bit of water to create steam from the fire, but not so much that it covers the oysters, fill the strainer basket

Traditionally, a fire pit is lit, a metal sheet is placed over the pit, and oysters are poured onto the metal sheet to cook over the open fire. We moisten burlap sacks with water, and use them to cover the oysters, which steams them as they cook. Watch the oysters to see when the shells pop open, indicating they are finished roasting.

full of oysters, place the basket in the pot, and cook them over the fire. It usually takes about 7 to 8 minutes per batch to cook them properly. And it's best to cook in batches to be sure the oysters are warm when enjoyed. Once they pop open, as I explained before, pour them out on tables covered with newspaper or paper cloths, and make sure everyone has the right utensils and sauces at hand.

The set-up is rustic, but standing at a waist-high table shucking hot oysters while talking and laughing with friends makes for a great party. When I was a child, my grandfather would use the spools from the electric company that the electric wire was wound upon. He would turn those sideways to make a table out of them. Of course, any table that can handle a wet environment is fine for an oyster roast.

Guests are provided with oyster knives and a light cotton glove (both these things are readily available at

kitchen stores, or on the internet) or dishcloth to hold the oyster as you pry it open. Some cooks like to provide simple aprons if a guest needs to protect their clothing. I've never been to a fancy-dress oyster roast, and my advice would be to dress casual and comfortable. When the oyster shell is pried open, the knife is then used to detach the oyster from the bottom shell, and you are ready to eat. Don't worry, the proper directions for shucking are included in this chapter (see p. 141).

You can eat oysters straight out of the shell, as Walt prefers, or on a cracker doused with spicy cocktail sauce. Horseradish is also a good condiment, and that's my personal preference. Discarded shells are gathered in the newspapers on the table, and new paper put out as needed. There's a ritual here, as you see.

Know that there are always two types of people at an oyster roast: those that love roasted oysters and those that don't. Some people don't like raw oysters and think that roasted oysters will taste the same as raw ones. Not true—they're better. I find it nice to offer a stew or chili to this group, without being judgmental. The Andouille Chili in this chapter is my favorite (and it's great for game days, too), and since these roasts are usually hosted in the cooler weather months, the warm bowl is welcomed.

How To Shuck An Oyster

WHAT YOU NEED:
gloves
oyster knives

1. Grab your oyster knife in the hand you write with, and pick up a towel or put a glove on the other hand. You will use your gloved hand to hold the oyster. Pick up your oyster with the cupped side down and flat side up. This keeps the "liquor" or liquid from the oyster from pouring out when you open it.

2. Look for the hinge of the oyster. This is where the two shells join together. It will be a curved area. Take the tip of your knife and place it in the hinge, or just next to it.

3. Once the tip of the knife is in, give the knife a 90-degree twist, and wiggle it gently until the hinge pops open.

4. With the two shells slightly separated, use your knife to lift the top flat shell away from the cupped bottom shell. The oyster and liquid will be in this bottom shell. The oyster liquor should be clear, never cloudy, and is really quite delicious.

5. Use your knife to cut the oyster from the bottom shell by running it underneath the oyster and disconnecting the muscle from the shell. Be sure not to scrape any shell fragments into the oyster shell—you don't want to eat them. Reserve the oyster liquid for the next step.

6. Now you can pick up your oyster and eat it on a cracker with hot sauce or horseradish, or any way you prefer. I like to drink the liquor that is left in the shell!

Roasted Oysters

An authentic oyster roast needs fire, metal, and oysters. That's it. Let's walk through the items needed, and how to use them. Here in Georgia, the oyster shells were traditionally used to made tabby, a historic building material still seen in many parts of the state.

Serves 5 to 6 oyster lovers

ITEMS YOU WILL NEED
1 bushel oysters
16 bricks
Firewood
Clean Shovel
Sheet metal, about 2-feet x 4-feet
2 buckets
2 burlap sacks
Oyster knives
Gloves
Rags (see p. 141)
Rustic table, to handle a wet
    environment

GARNISH
Saltine crackers
Fresh lemons wedges
Horseradish sauce
Tabasco sauce
Cocktail sauce (recipe, p. 53)

First, rinse your oysters. I recommend pouring them out on a large table. You want to clean off any extra mud without soaking them, because soaking them will reduce the flavor. Give them a good rinse with your water hose. They will be wet when you cook them, and that's okay. They came from the sea!

In a separate bucket, soak 1 to 2 burlap sacks in fresh water.

In order to cook the oysters, you will need to make a fire pit with a piece of sturdy sheet metal on top. The metal should be sturdy enough to hold 15 to 20 pounds of oysters at a time. Stack 4 stacks of 3 to 4 bricks for the legs to hold the sheet metal. These stacks will comprise the four corners of the fire pit, and will give you enough height to work the fire beneath the metal.

Build and light your fire, and cover with the sheet metal. Let the fire get a strong start and burn down a bit. Just as the fire starts to slow, test the metal to see if it will create steam. Grab a handful of water and throw it on the metal. If it evaporates into steam quickly, you are ready to cook.

Take about ⅓ of your rinsed bushel of oysters and pour out evenly on top of the hot metal. Try not to stack the oysters on top of each other, so they will cook more evenly. Cover the raw oysters with the wet burlap sack. This will create a steaming effect on the oysters.

Let the oysters cook for about 7 to 8 minutes under the sack. Watch for them to begin popping open. Once they do, remove each with a long spatula, or a clean shovel, used only for cooking. Scoop them into a clean bucket, and pour out onto a serving table to enjoy immediately.

Make sure to have oyster knives, and gloves with rags on the table to shuck the oysters.

Repeat 2 to 3 more times until all the oysters are eaten.

Oysters can be eaten alone, or atop a Saltine cracker with your choice of garnishes.

Andouille Chili

Tracy Stickley introduced me to the value of adding Andouille sausage to chili. I tried hers, and never looked back. You can omit this step, and double up the ground beef. However, I would give it a try, at least once. Be sure to let your chili simmer for at least 30 minutes before serving. Additionally, you can make this the day ahead and refrigerate it in a covered container until ready to serve. Be sure to reheat it slowly, as it will scorch! This chili can also be frozen in an airtight container for an easy dinner, or a meal to take to a friend in a pinch. And the McCormick chili packets are a great way to start your seasoning. Don't be afraid to get a little help if it moves the dish along. You are still the chef, even with McCormick's aid!

Serves 12, but can be halved

2 pounds Andouille sausage, sliced in bite-sized rounds
2 pounds lean ground beef
2 teaspoons salt
2 cups coarsely chopped yellow onion
2 tablespoons chopped garlic
2 quarts Kitchen Basics Salted Beef Stock
2 (30-ounce) cans diced tomatoes
2 (30-ounce) cans crushed tomatoes
4 McCormick Chili packets
1 teaspoon garlic powder
1 teaspoon chili powder
½ teaspoon cayenne (optional)
Salt and Pepper to taste

OPTIONAL GARNISH
Shredded cheese
Green onions
Sour cream

Brown the sausage slices in a big stock pot over medium-high heat for 3 to 5 minutes until lightly browned. Transfer the slices to a paper towel-lined plate to drain.

In the same pot, brown the ground beef with the salt, breaking up the chunks with a wooden spoon and stirring to brown evenly. Drain any extra fat, and use a slotted spoon to transfer the ground beef into a separate bowl.

Next, add the chopped onion to the pot, and cook on medium-high for 6 to 8 minutes, until it begins to look translucent and the edges turn brown. Lower the heat to medium, add the chopped garlic, and cook for two minutes, or until fragrant.

After two minutes, pour in the beef stock to deglaze the pan, scraping the bottom of the pot to get all the good bits. Add the crushed tomatoes, diced tomatoes, and the browned meat to the pot, and lower the heat to medium-low to bring everything to a slow simmer.

To season, stir in the McCormick Chili packets, garlic powder, and cayenne pepper. Test, and add salt and pepper to taste. Continue to simmer on low for 30 minutes, stirring often.

Serve hot and garnish with your choice of shredded cheese, green onions, and sour cream.

Sweet Jalapeño Cornbread Muffins

I was inspired to make these by the cornbread served at Ripe Thing Market in Greensboro, Georgia. It is a great dual restaurant and grocery store. They have daily specials, sandwiches, and a wonderful produce and meat selection. All of their homemade soups come with a slice of cornbread, and I prefer the jalapeño variety. But what makes Ripe Thing so great is Mr. Ken, the owner and chef. He knows all of his customers, including me, our children, and our dogs. He asks about our parties, our food, and what's going on in our lives. Plus, he is a talented chef who hails from High Cotton in Charleston, South Carolina. These cornbread muffins are inspired by his friendship, and what this book is all about—Southern hospitality and goodness.

Makes 1 dozen muffins

1 egg
1 cup buttermilk
2 cups self-rising buttermilk cornmeal mix
⅔ cup sugar
⅓ cup diced pickled jalapeños, plus more for serving

Preheat the oven to 425 degrees F.

Combine all ingredients in a large mixing bowl, and stir until the batter is well mixed.

Spray a 12-muffin tin with Baker's Joy.

Spoon 3 tablespoons of the cornbread mixture into each muffin cup.

Bake for 15 to 18 minutes until golden brown, and a toothpick placed in the middle of one comes out clean.

Lemon Layers

My Granny Cheney called these Lemon Layers in her personal cookbook, and I just love that name. She learned the recipe from Ruth Howell, "Munner" as she was affectionately called. Munner attended Branford Presbyterian Church in Branford, Florida, with my granny when my mother was growing up. Munner was known to host the ladies of the church on many occasions, and serve these very lemon treats. If Munner were alive today, she would be nearly 150 years old. The original recipe called for 4 tablespoons of lemon juice. But Granny mentioned she always added more, so I included 6.

Note: A knife dipped in water will help to cut these so that they come out with clean edges.

Yields about 16 squares

BOTTOM LAYER
½ cup butter, room temperature
1 cup all-purpose flour
¼ cup powdered sugar

TOP LAYER
1 cup sugar
2 tablespoons flour
½ teaspoon baking soda
2 eggs, lightly beaten
6 tablespoons fresh lemon juice
1 to 2 tablespoons powdered sugar

Preheat your oven 350 degrees F.

Spray a 9-inch square pan with Baker's Joy.

To make the Bottom layer, mix all the ingredients, and use your hands to press the dough into the bottom of the square pan. Bake this layer for 15 minutes.

While this is baking, prepare the the top layer.

Combine the sugar, flour, baking soda, eggs, and lemon juice in a mixing bowl and stir until everything is well incorporated.

Pour over the warm, baked bottom layer, and bake for 25 minutes. After removing from the oven, and while the lemon layers are still warm, sprinkle with the powdered sugar. Let the pan cool before cutting into squares.

You don't need to refrigerate them to enjoy, but if you refrigerate for a couple of hours, they will firm up and are easier to cut into clean squares.

Index

Page numbers in italics indicate illustrations

Resource Guide

Bayou Classic
601-591-1350, www.bayouclassic.com
4-gallon Stainless Bayou® Fryer, for deep-frying
fish, hushpuppies, or pork chops.

Cuisinart
www.cuisinart.com
Automatic Frozen Yogurt-Ice Cream and Sorbet
Maker. Convenient 2-quart ice cream maker for
making ice cream and other cold treats with ease.

Hardy Farms
888-368-NUTS, www.hardyfarmspeanuts.com
1659 Eastman Highway
Hawkinsville, Georgia 31036
Fresh Georgia peanuts sold at the main location,
or in fruit stands along the central and
southwest corridor of Georgia, or online.

Lee's Bees Honey
478-288-3052, email: leepamelar@gmail.com
Eatonton, Georgia
Local Eatonton honey, harvested by Pam and Bill
Lee, from over 50 hives.

Louisiana Crawfish Company
318-379-0539, www.lacrawfish.com
140 Russell Cemetery Road
Natchitoches, Louisiana 71457
Fresh Crawfish to your door in 24 hours,
or order frozen in the off season.

Pearson Farm
888-423-7374, www.pearsonfarm.com
5575 Zenith Mill Road
Fort Valley, Georgia 31030
Family farm, owned since 1885, for all your fresh
Georgia peaches and pecans.

Ripe Thing Market
706-454-2155, on Facebook, or
email: ripethingmarketga@gmail.com
112 West Broad Street
Greensboro, Georgia 30642
Local lunch deli and a daily market, with Chow
Chow relish, fresh fruit and vegetables, grass-fed
beef, and a variety of homemade regional fare.

Southern Flavoring Company
www.southernflavoring.com
Features baking extracts and flavoring, including
Happy Home Imitation Butter and Nut flavoring.
Also available at Amazon.com.

Acknowledgments

Thank you to the army of people who helped me in the process of the development of this book. Of course to Walt, for loving me and helping me to come back to myself, to us, to our family.

For our dear sweet children for coming along with us on this journey of life, for bringing abounding joy, and filling our lives with precious moments.

To my parents, Cynthia and Eddie DeLoach, for your steadfast love and encouragement to always believe in our dreams. And especially to my mother for making my life and the tablespaces in this book beautiful. To Rebecca and Mr. Rocker for knowing how to fry fish, so I could fall in love with Walt, and especially for loving me as a part of this family that I have grown to call my own.

To Grandmother Virginia DeLoach, for the daily inspirations and countless conversations about lasting memories and defining recipes of my childhood. To my Granny Avis Cheney in heaven, for having the wisdom and foresight to write down her treasured memories and favorite foods while she was still with us.

To Janice Shay, my editor, producer, and friend, for teaching and helping me bring this book to life, and for making the food look good enough to lick right off the page. To Roxy and Jim Stone, for your friendship and for photographing almost all of the most important events of our lives, including this book.

To Candace Couch, my therapist, for assigning me the work to "write the book," and helping me to see the world in a more compassionate and loving way.

To Jenny Byrd, writer and college roommate extraordinaire, for being one of my first confidants about this idea and encouraging me to finish.

To Latham Foster, Pam Lee, and Taylor Prestridge for cooking up a storm in the kitchen while we photographed these many recipes. To my Aunt Susan Cheney, Aunt Pam Huff, and Aunt Patty Onorato for continuing the traditions of our families in the kitchen and in our lives, so I could follow and learn. To Aunt Holly Parker for your artistic inspiration and encouragement, and of course, your gourds and beautiful artwork. To Uncle Lou Cason for teaching me how to make the best deviled eggs. To my cousin, Lynn Tootle, for teaching me how to properly set up a Low Country Boil. To Marie and Cooper Rainey for allowing me to share one of the stories of your lives to inspire the lives of others. To Tracy Stickley and Sandy Dillard for sharing your recipe secrets so I could share them in this book. To Kathy Murphy for helping us keep our lives in order. To Jamey Williamson for finding doves to enjoy. To Joe Tkacik for taking the most awesome Halloween House picture ever.

Thank you to everyone I spoke to about this book and replied, "How exciting! We can't wait to read it!" Your encouragement and enthusiasm helped me to believe this book was meant to be. And, to all of you who I listened to in person, online, through podcasts, and in books about the courageous battle of mental health, thank you for giving me, and the rest of the world, hope.

A final word: The recipes in this book are good for family and friends, and for virtually any get-together. Just remember to include your children and grandchildren when you plan. One day they just might write a book about you!

Photos opposite, clockwise from upper left: Eleanor Rocker and Latham Foster; Ken McCord; Cynthia DeLoach; Ford Rocker; Virginia DeLoach; Taylor Prestridge; Tara Rocker and Eddie DeLoach; Pam Lee; and (center) Isabelle Rocker.

If you or someone you know is suffering from depression,
reach out to a trusted family member, counselor,
or chaplin. You can also text or call 988,
the Suicide and Crisis lifeline of 988lifeline.org.
The world is a better place with you in it.